LANGUAGE OF THE AXIS

LANGUAGE OF THE AXIS

Mary O'Donnell Fulkerson

ARTS ARCHIVES

THEATRE PAPERS
THE FIRST SERIES 1977-78

Arts Documentation Unit
Exeter EX4 6JA, UK
Dir: Peter Hulton

Published in this edition in 2025 by:
Triarchy Press
Axminster, England

info@triarchypress.net
www.triarchypress.net

Copyright © Arts Documentation Unit, U.K. 2004 and 2025

The right of Mary Fulkerson to be identified as the author of this work has been asserted by them in accordance with the Copyright, Designs and Patents Act, 1988.

No part of this publication may be reproduced, stored in a retrieval system or transmitted in any form or by any means including photocopying, electronic, mechanical, recording or otherwise, without the prior written permission of the publisher.

All rights reserved.

A catalogue record for this book is available from the British Library.

Print ISBN: 978-1-913743-95-6
ePub ISBN: 978-1-913743-96-3

The photographs were taken in 1975 by Brian Haslem during movement sessions taught by Mary O'Donnell Fulkerson at Dartington College of Arts in Totnes, Devon, UK.

Mary O'Donnell Fulkerson, c. 1978. Photographer unknown.

Preface

Language of the Axis was written and illustrated by the American dancer and teacher Mary O'Donnell Fulkerson on her arrival in 1973 from the United States at Dartington College of Arts – an innovative Arts Education Centre based in Devon, UK which was later to offer undergraduate degree programmes within an expanding and socially committed field of arts practice.

Fulkerson came from the post-Cunningham reformulation of dance and movement practice occurring in the USA at the time – promoted by, among others, the Judson Dance Theatre, Anna Halprin, Yvonne Rainer and Simone Forte, along with movement practitioners such as Barbara Clark, Joan Skinner and Nancy Topf. The direction was towards a closer investigation of the body and its relationship with thought and imagery – both as performance and as experience.

Of her solo 'Real Adventures' *The New York Times* in 1984 wrote: "One had a sudden vision of Diaghilev's surprise as he watched Dalcroze's strange music-explorations, or of Isadora Duncan's early audiences as they saw her embody music."

Fulkerson's pedagogical work was termed Release Technique. At Dartington she was responsible for inviting Sir Richard Alston, the American dancers Steve Paxton, Katie Duck and others, to come and join her and their work, together with the annual dance festivals she organised, were particularly influential in the development of New Dance in the UK.

In 1989, Fulkerson moved to the Netherlands and co-founded, with Aat Hougée, the Center for New Dance Development (CNDO) in Arnhem, later renamed the European Dance Development Center (EDDC). Throughout her years of teaching, writing and performing her students fanned out to make a wide variety of societal contributions, both in the UK and Europe, as professional choreographers, community dance activists, movement teachers and therapists.

She later returned to Austin, Texas to be near her son and died there in 2020. Her enduring attention to the body in its operation with imagery might well prove of increasing interest in the age of Artificial Intelligence.

Contents

Preface vii

Part One: A LOOK AT THE BODY 1

Part Two: EASY ACTION 71

Part Three: SEEING A CONTEXT 113

About *Theatre Papers* 128

Part One: 'A Look at the Body' is a series of drawings describing the body. These are based upon an anatomical understanding of how bones balance in correct body alignment and of how muscles function in groups.

Part Two: 'Easy Action' is a series of specific movements which provide an opportunity to use and experience the body descriptions in action. Each action is described in detail so that the interior of the action becomes clear.

Part Three: 'Seeing a Context' is about the use of these materials. The author's personal experience of these images and actions provides examples of their use.

This writing is about the integration of mind and body. Thought and action together produce the whole self and neither can exist in isolation from the other. In order to use thought and action together a new language is employed. This is the language of the axis, not a language of words, but of experienced sensation. The parts of the body are in continual conversation with one another and with the world. The discovery and practice of this conversation form the subject of this writing.

PART ONE: A LOOK AT THE BODY

Developing a Language of Body Images

Every person has some idea of their body, of how it looks, how it is shaped, how long and how wide. These body ideas are constructed from all kinds of suggestions which one usually fails to sift through and select. Some of the things one might suggest to the body, perhaps how it should look and be, are inaccurate and even detrimental. However, these suggestions are rarely examined, and bodies suffer as a result.

By making a close survey of the body one can begin to revise body ideas. In order to think easily about the body, anatomical information can be formed into simple thoughts which imply physical sensations that occur when the body is being used properly. These thoughts are full of implication for the whole body. They are the anatomical images.

A body image is an idea about the body that facilitates easy action, which comes when the spread of body information from one body part to another is encouraged. Such an image gives to the body the physical information which helps the muscles to direct the way bones balance in action. A body image can become very strong through concentrated work and can finally be incorporated within the body.

Real physical change can result from concentration over a period of time working with images that are anatomically correct. The body is available for change if change is encouraged and allowed. Thus the physical information which is being spoken silently throughout the body forms the language of the axis. Body images do the speaking.

LINES IN THE BODY

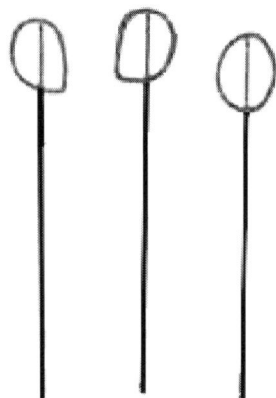

The Centre Line

Balance the body around a central, vertical line, a central, vertical axis.

Balancing standing

The vertebral column approximates the central, vertical axis in the torso.

Balancing sitting

In Line: Shoulder, Elbow, Wrist, Second Finger

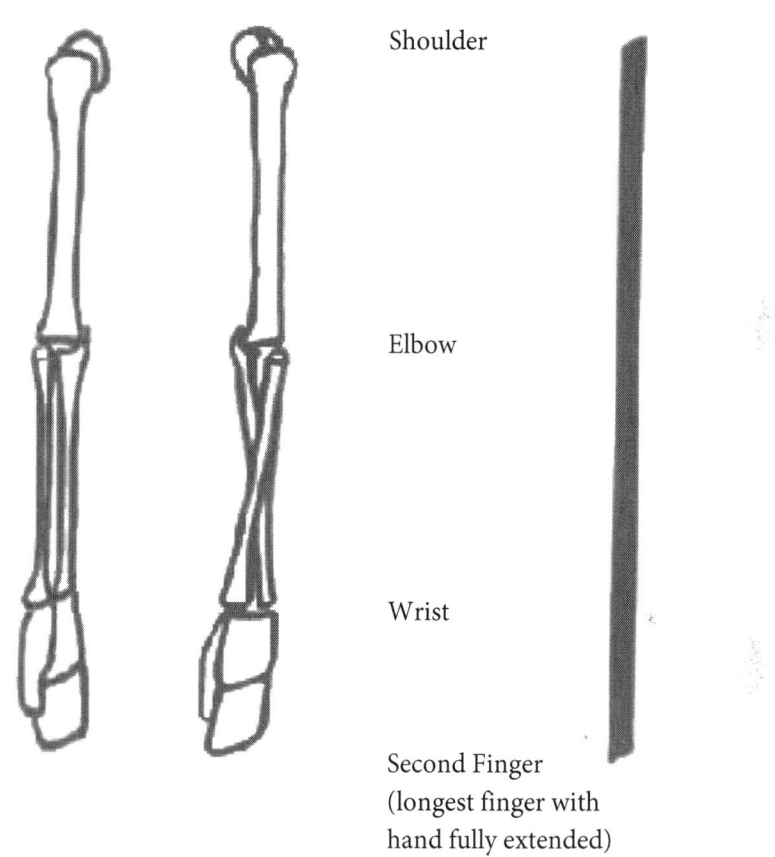

Shoulder

Elbow

Wrist

Second Finger
(longest finger with
hand fully extended)

In Line: Hip, Knee, Ankle, Second Toe

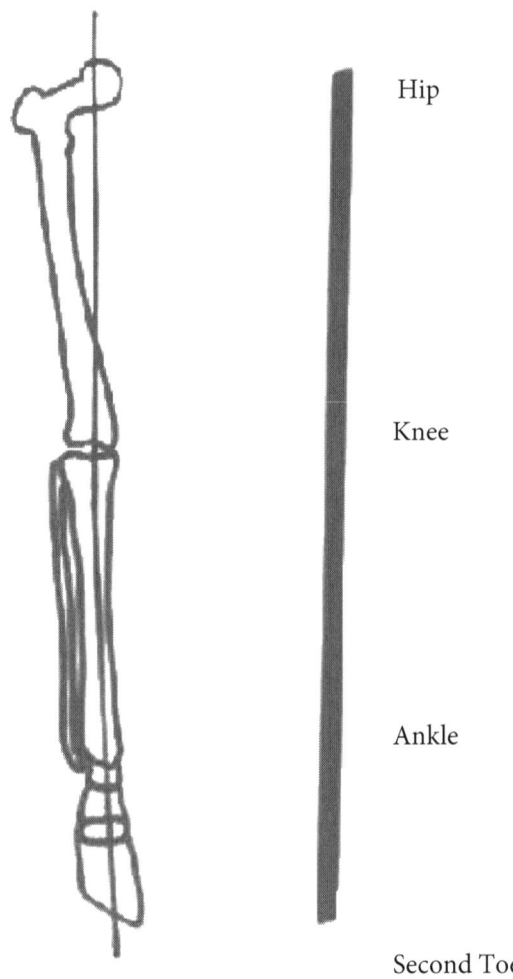

Hip

Knee

Ankle

Second Toe

BRIDGES IN THE BODY

Information passes across the body from one side to the other and from front to back.

Foot Bridge

The bones of the foot form a bridge which carries information from the heel to the toes.

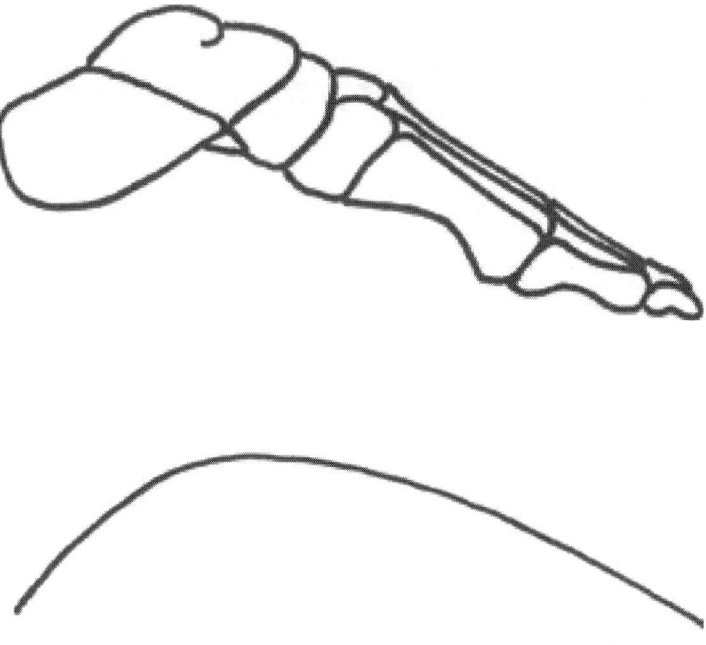

Images Come from Anatomical Understanding

Bones fall in the body because of their weight. In any body position the bones either balance in the body like a tower of building blocks or else they hang like a pendulum. The muscles direct the way to balance or swing the bones. Muscles pass the total body weight into the bones which balance to support the body in any one movement.

The following images are simplified pictures of muscles and bones. Sometimes they refer to action based upon muscle action and the function of bone meeting bone. Sometimes they refer to alignment, that is, the normal relationships of bones and muscles in the body. Occasionally the images refer to the way the whole body works as a unit. These images deal with a total body state.

Bridges in Legs

Information passes from leg to leg across a muscular bridge which goes from the top of each upper thigh bone to the lower one-third of the vertebral column. This bridge is deep inside the body. Legs also pass information to each other across the bottom back of the vertebral column.

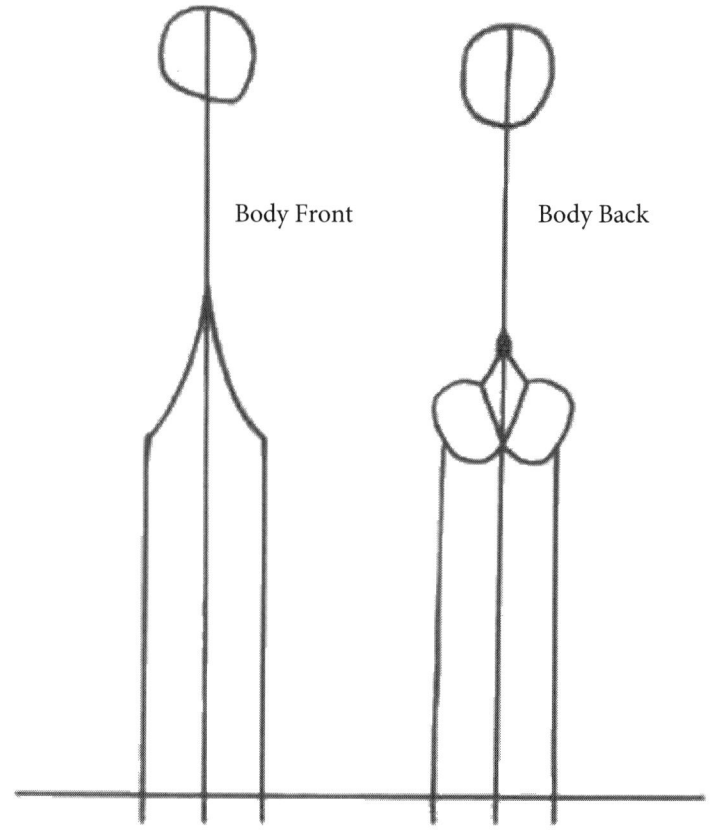

Body Front   Body Back

Bridges in Arms

Muscles connect each shoulder to every bone in the vertebral column, down the whole back of the body and up into the neck. These muscles form a bridge of information from one arm to another. A different set of muscles connects each shoulder to the centre of the chest. There is another bridge from arm to arm across the front of the body.

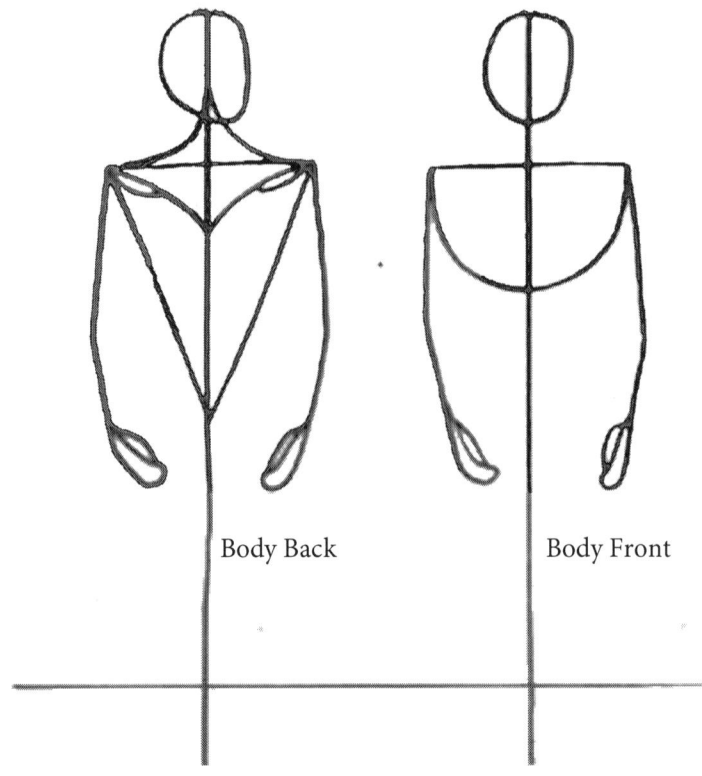

Body Back   Body Front

From Thought into Action

Think the image first, then let simple actions follow from the image. The point upon which attention is centred becomes important. An easy action like crawling can tell one something about the vertebral column, something about leg action, something about arm, shoulder and hip action. It can tell one something about many different things. Centring attention upon any one of these ideas can develop physical thought. It can integrate the idea and the act.

See it.
Think it.
Forget it.
Then it happens.

Finally the images become part of physical thought. The images themselves are forgotten and fully known. Each image is relevant to every simple action. Each image is to be learned in order that it becomes part of mind and body intelligence and forgotten.

The image suggests movement to the body and the body responds. The image is considered as part of the whole-body context. It is essential, but not manipulative; it is dominant because of its total absorption throughout the body. To forget the image means that the whole body is moving in a responsive state which has been formed from the image itself.

Seeing Stillness

The repetition of an image leads to action, though this does not happen immediately. Long stillnesses characterise this work. This kind of involvement is apparent to some who watch the process but is not always apparent to everyone. The action of looking can include the process of seeing thought happen in another person. It is useful to remember that both stillness and watching are dynamic activities.

Bridge between Arms and Legs

Two bridges intersect low in the centre of the body. Arm action travels down back of vertebral column. Leg action travels up front of vertebral column.

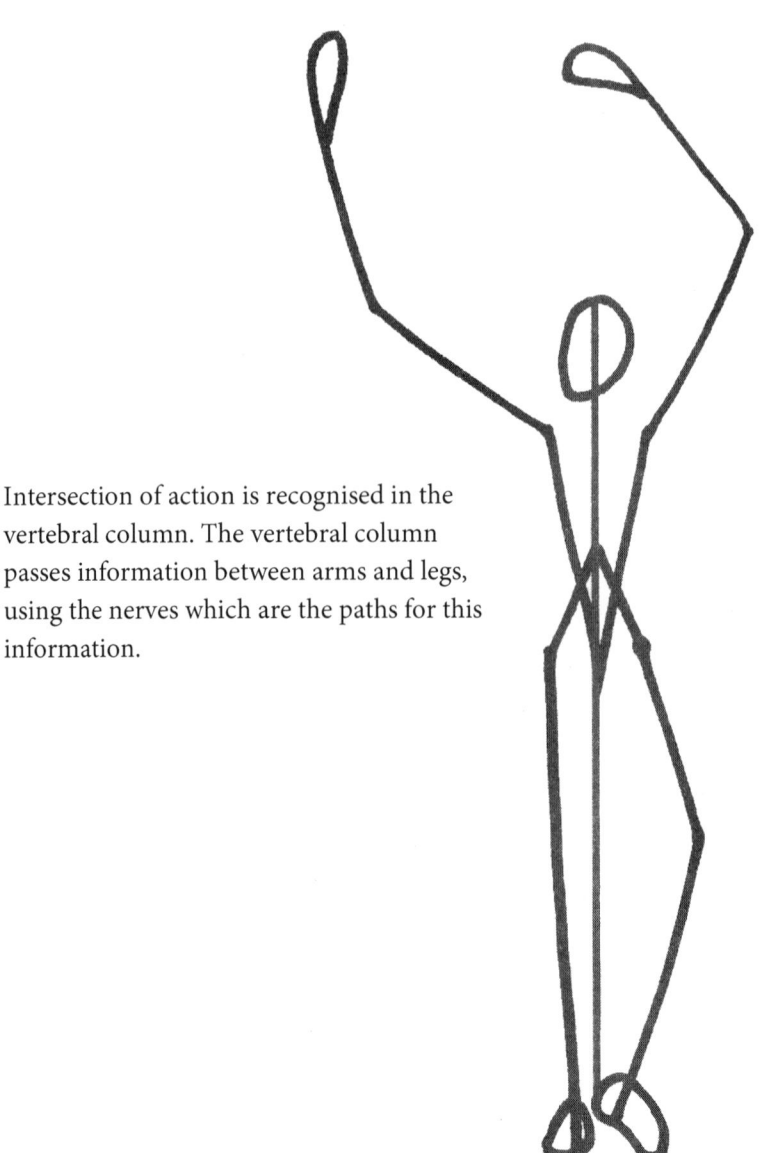

Intersection of action is recognised in the vertebral column. The vertebral column passes information between arms and legs, using the nerves which are the paths for this information.

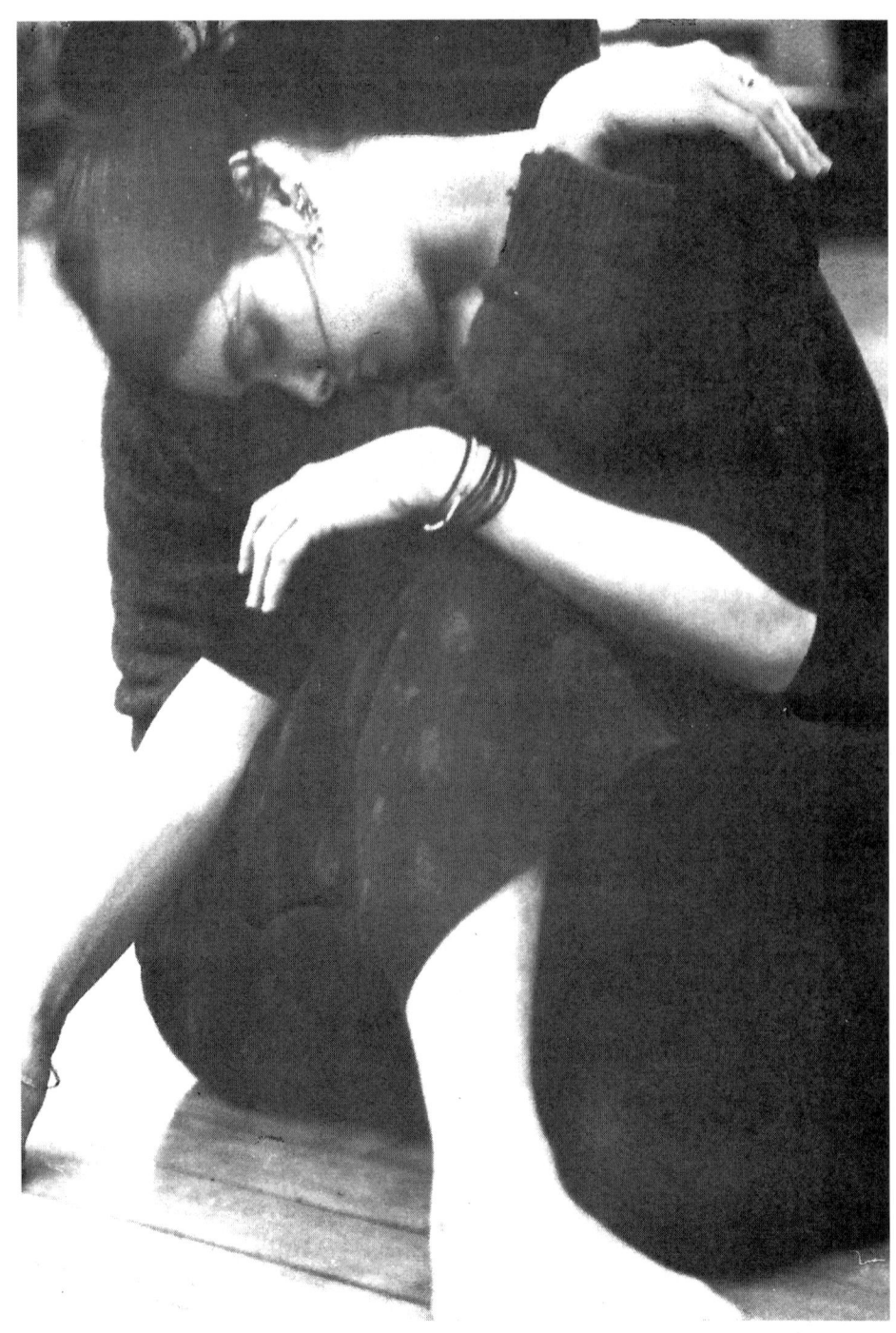

BOWLS IN THE BODY

Bowl in Shoulders

A bowl shape is formed in the shoulder region by the sternum (long bone in centre front of upper torso between ribs, runs vertically for six to ten inches), clavicles (collar bones), scapulae (shoulder blades), and muscles connecting scapulae to the vertebral column. The structure is circular and supportive, giving leverage to upper torso, head and arms. Let shoulder basin give stability to action in head, neck, arms and shoulders.

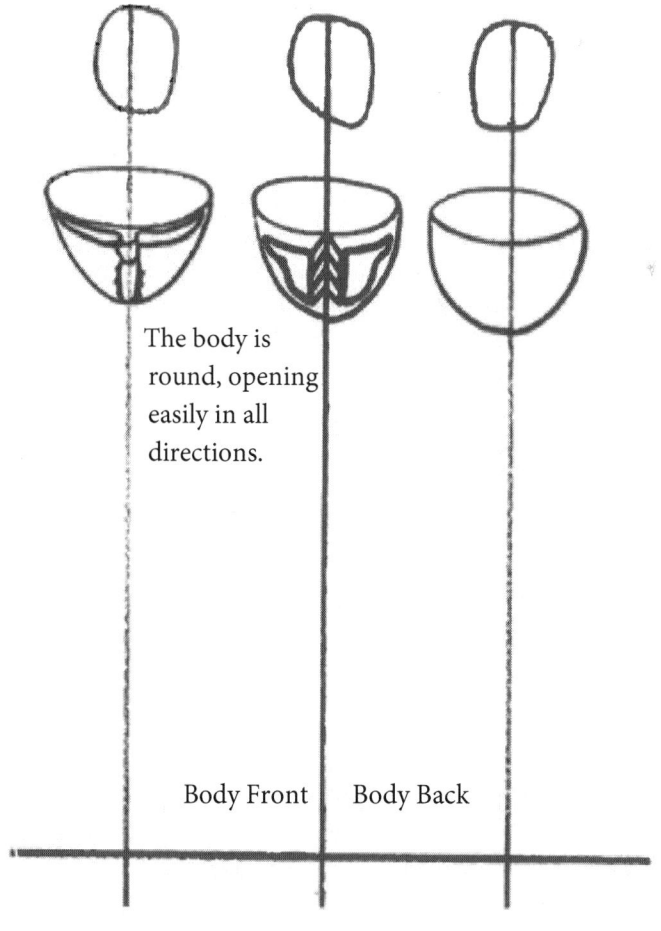

The body is round, opening easily in all directions.

Body Front   Body Back

Working with a Body Image

A body image such as a bridge translates a physical understanding of the construction of the body into sensory experience. Such an image relates the body to the world; for example, when the body weight transfers itself over the arch of a foot, one can experience the real sensation of crossing a bridge.

The selection of an image is the first step towards working with a body image. The image is then made the centre of attention. The image is recalled on every breath-out whilst the image falls out of conscious thought on the breath-in. First one thinks the image and then the image rests. The body remains still until action is demanded from the image itself. This might take time. A low energy plateau is reached. As the work proceeds, this low energy plateau is redefined and can be deepened simply by repeated practice. Finally, the image no longer alternates between working and resting but becomes a forgotten source, a unity of body and thought. One no longer thinks the image but becomes it. To forget the image is to allow one to become the image.

An imagined journey begins with the feeling of axial movement in the body. Specific movements can be learned and used. The image strongly directs activity. One forgets to think the image and it exists within the person. One surrenders to the image. The image rolls, stands, turns, curves, folds, opens, walks, falls and rests the body. Across and through space the image compels movement. One passes easily from unity of the whole body to small detail. As the whole body works harmoniously, all parts are expressed in one another. Action and image interplay. New images emerge. Feelings, dreams, memories and associations present their aspects and fall away. In this work technique is defined as the integration of idea and act and it is the result of the persistent dialogue between demand and patience.

Bowl in Hips

A bowl shape is formed by the bones of the pelvis which make a complete circle around the bottom of the torso. This bowl supports the action of the whole torso and stabilises the action of the legs. Shoulder and leg bowls are really open at the bottom but are given the images of bowls to make it easier to experience the supporting nature of the structures.

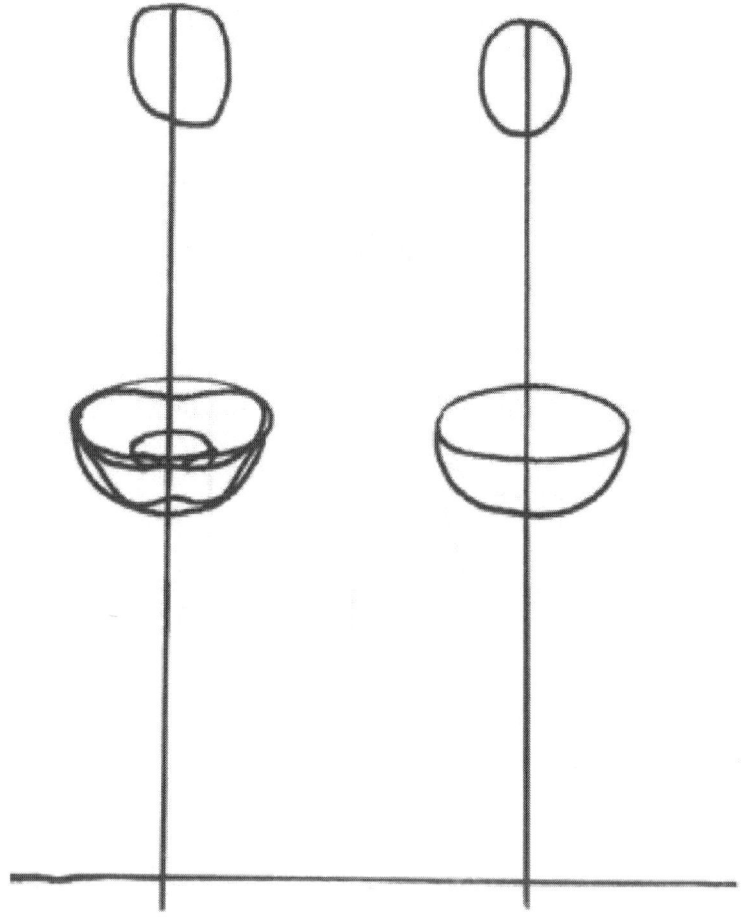

Bowls in Shoulders and Hips

Two bowls work together. When the body is balanced around the vertical axis both bowls are balanced and if filled with water would not spill any. When the torso bends, twists, curves, folds towards the legs, these bowls empty and refill.

Two bowls support the torso.

Sitting

Standing

SPHERES IN THE BODY

Hand and Foot

The hand rests around a sphere.
The foot rests over two spheres

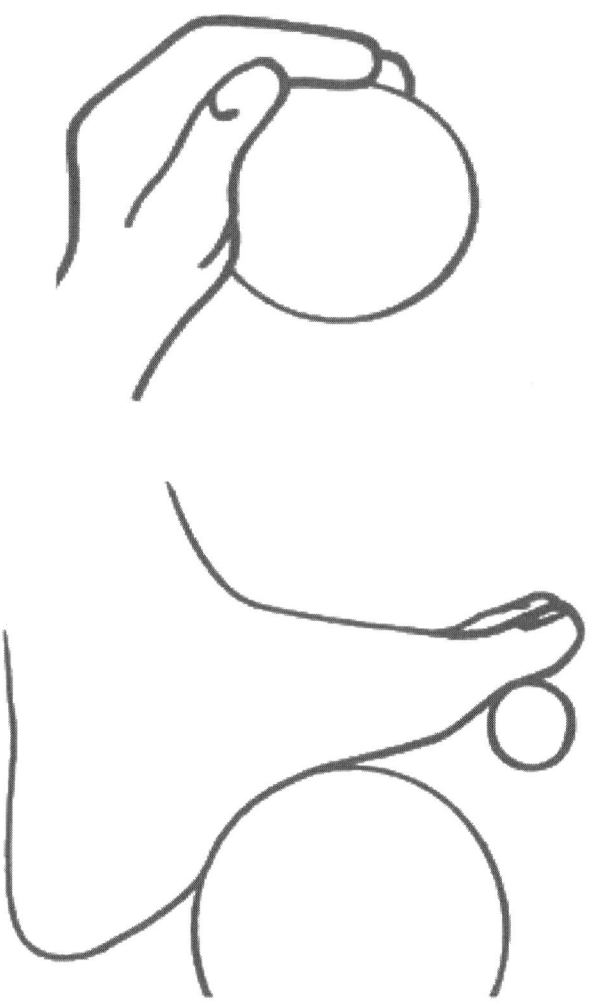

Hands

Two hands know each other around a sphere.

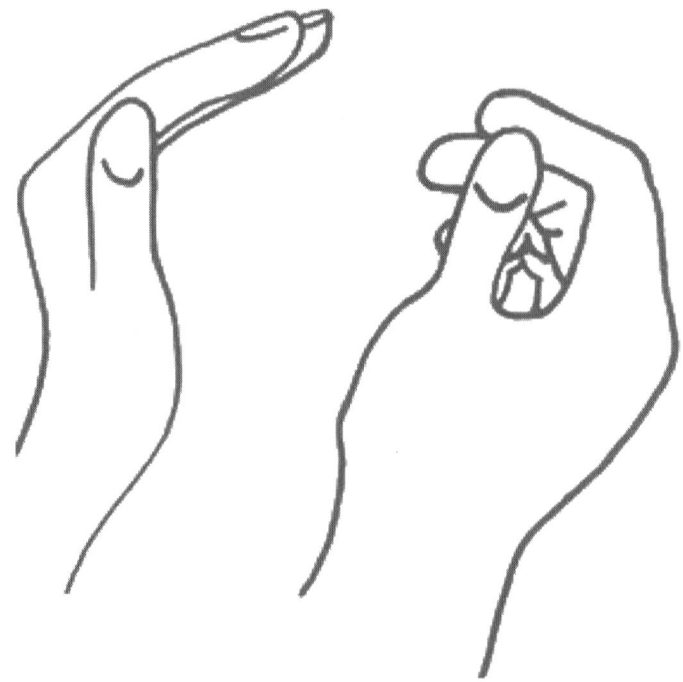

The centre of the whole body, the vertical axis, speaks throughout the body. Each part of the body participates in the knowledge of the central vertical axis. All the shapes of the body are known and expressed in all the body parts. Ordered forms are repeated throughout.

Using Breath with Images and Actions

The breath becomes important when using these images. A passive use of the breath allows the breath to function normally. So long as breathing continues easily in movement or stillness, the natural rhythm can be observed. See breath without affecting breath rhythm. Listen to breathing.

The active use of breath with action requires controlling the breath and action together so that the two achieve agreement. There are two possibilities. These may seem contradictory, but they can be complementary, each satisfying different demands.

Breathe out as the folding action brings the body parts together, and breathe in as lengthening takes the body parts into long lines.

Or, breathe in as a preparation for action and breathe out on the execution of the action.

In general, softness and fluidity are achieved by passive use of the breath – just by listening or by breathing out on folding or breathing in on lengthening. For heavy or strong actions demanding high energy and speed, the breath-in on preparation and the breath-out on execution is the most useful way to work.

When one begins to work with an image, the listening to breathing can provide a body rhythm that allows the image to enter thought repeatedly. This repetition unites the thinking process with the body rhythm of breath. With thought rhythm and body rhythm functioning together, thinking easily finds the rhythm of action. Thought becomes action.

Breathe in and rest the image. Let it escape thought. Breathe out and create the image in thought, in the body- deep thinking of the image. Breath can add definition, force, clarity and fluidity and it provides a fundamental, basic body rhythm. The body demands changes in the breath. This is an automatic action. Changes in body energy cause breath changes. To listen to the changes in breath rhythms gives information about the interior of the body. Working with the breath brings to consciousness the work going on inside the body all the time.

The yawn is the deepest of breaths.

BREATH

The Continuous Thread

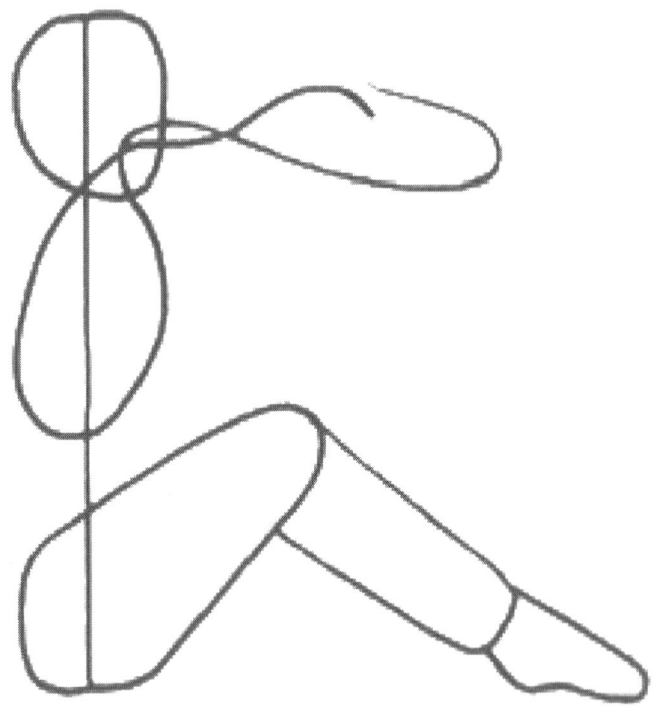

Breath is a continuous thread.
Breath-in flows into breath-out.

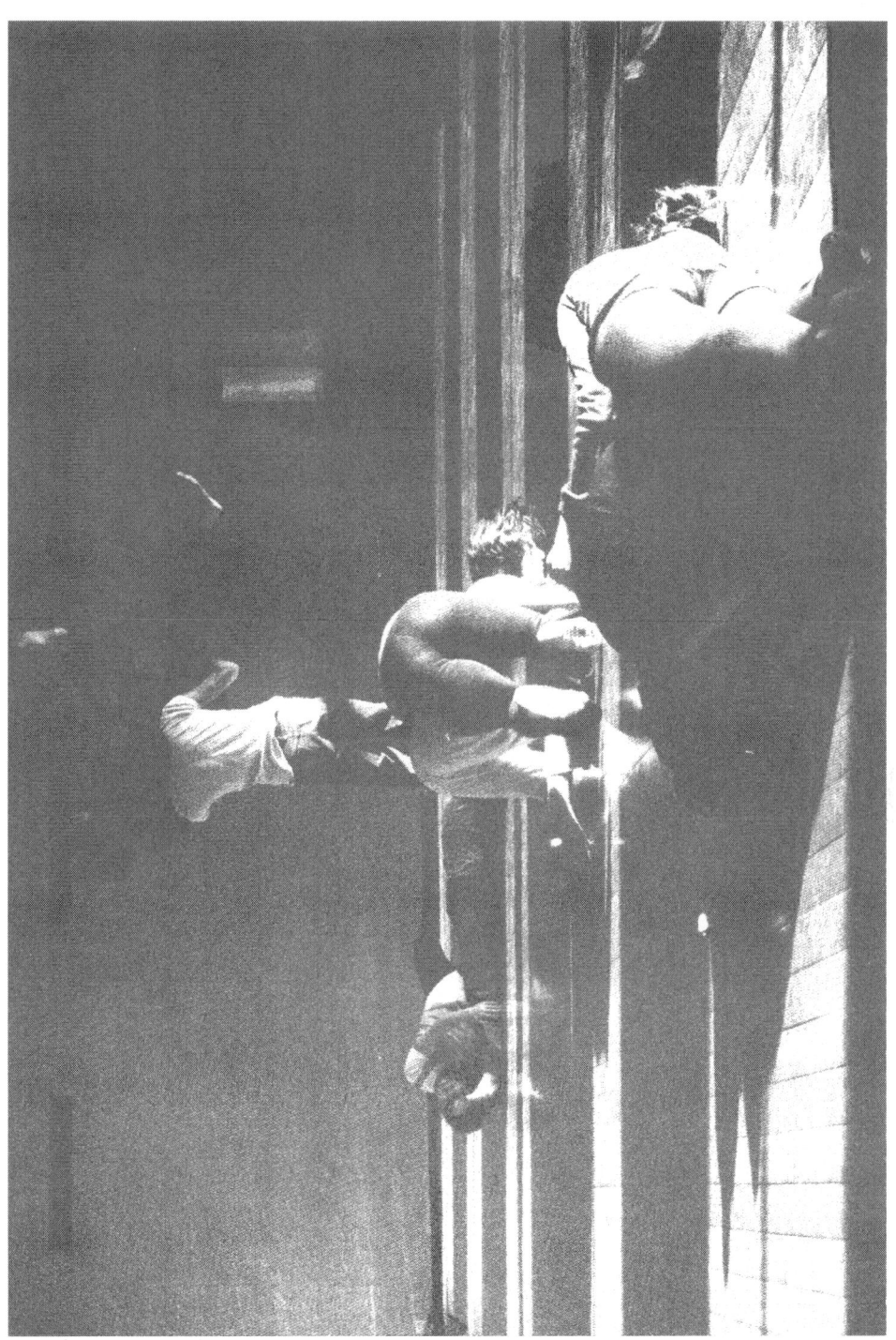

Yawn

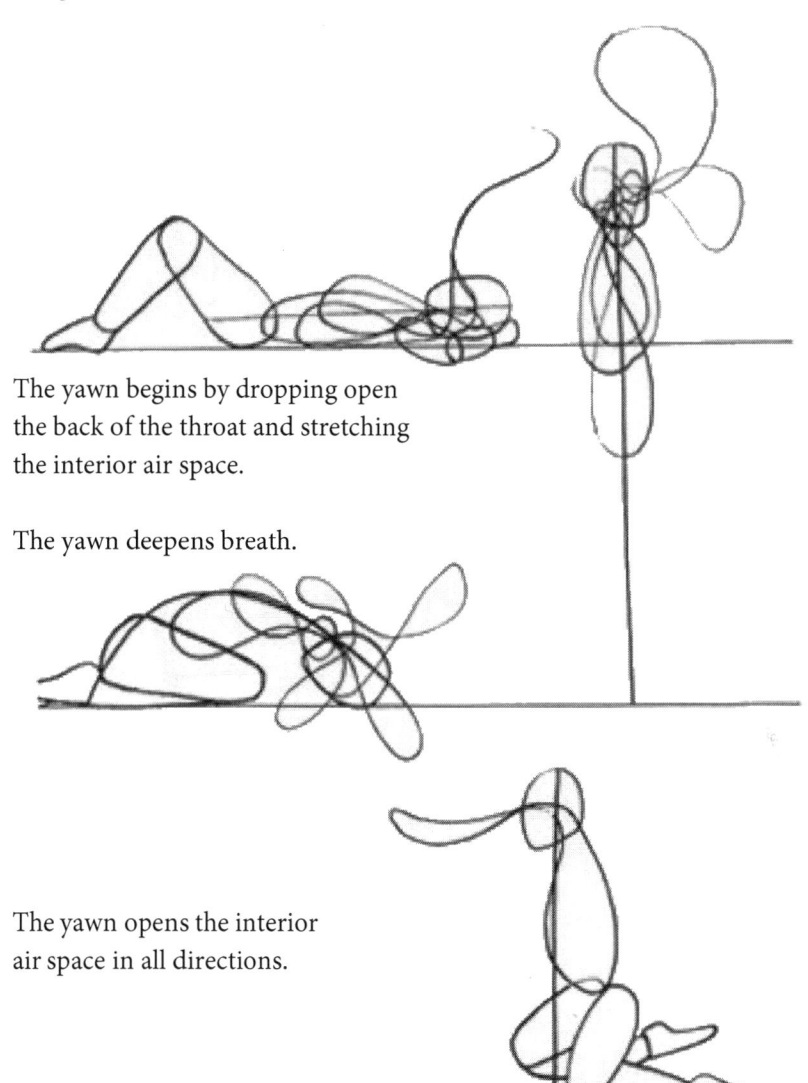

The yawn begins by dropping open the back of the throat and stretching the interior air space.

The yawn deepens breath.

The yawn opens the interior air space in all directions.

The Yawn Centres the Mandible

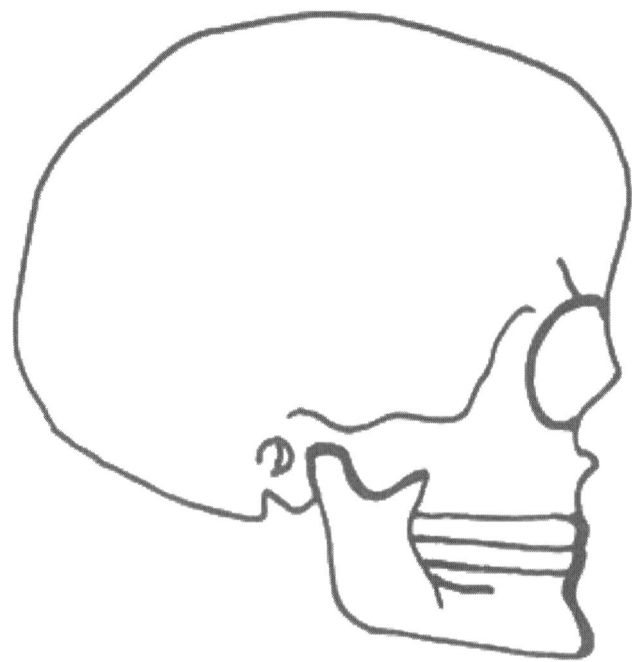

The end of a yawn centres the jaw bone (mandible) into its sockets immediately in front of each ear on both sides of the head.

A Moving Image

The body parts balance as weights in the body. This is a dynamic balance with weights continually shifting and with muscles adjusting bones to form new supports.

Action passes throughout the body as the muscles direct bones to take the shifting weight.

Action flows easily in the body when the weights pass smoothly where the weight is shared across joints and when the balance of the body parts is made easy.

Some body images describe the flow of action in the body, the shifting of weight, the dynamic balances.

Informing Reason

The body resists the change that is forced upon it. Usually the body does what it is told. If the body is asked by reason to go to the door, the body goes to the door. If the body is asked to sit down, the body sits. Occasionally the body asks something. Being tired, wanting food, these are common questions coming from the body which are normally thought of as needs because of their unmistakable and urgent nature. But the body is asking and frequently is not heard. The body is continually giving information, and the way the body gives information to reason is often as a result of the particular questions the body itself is asking. Discomfort in the body, even if it is habitual, as in the case of poor posture, affects perception. How the world appears is a result of this dialogue between the body needs and the world.

So, the body is doing what it is told, but often it is giving information and asking questions that relate to the interior which is rarely perceived.

ACTION FLOWS DOWN THE BACK; UP THE FRONT

The Vertebrae

Each vertebra becomes centred by allowing the front of the vertebra (vertebral body) to float upward and by allowing the back of the vertebra (spinous process) to lower downward. The whole vertebral column rises in the front and lowers in the back, achieving greater length.

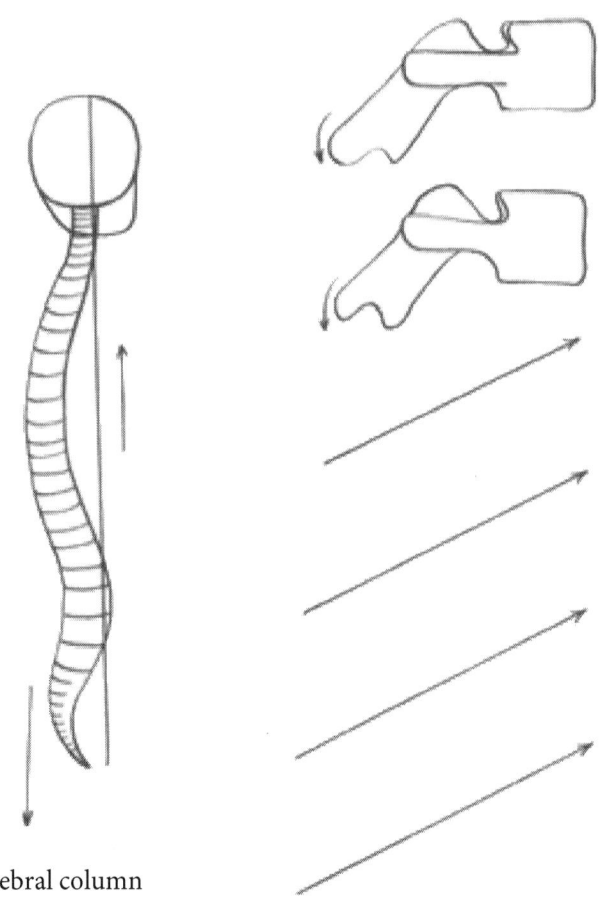

Side of vertebral column

Line of action for vertebrae

The Pelvis

Action flows down the back of the pelvis and up the front. The sacrum at the base of the vertebral column forms the back of the pelvic bowl. As the sacrum is lowered, the vertebral column becomes longer. As the back of the pelvis drops, the front of the pelvis rises and this action forms the support for the abdominal muscles rising up the front of the torso.

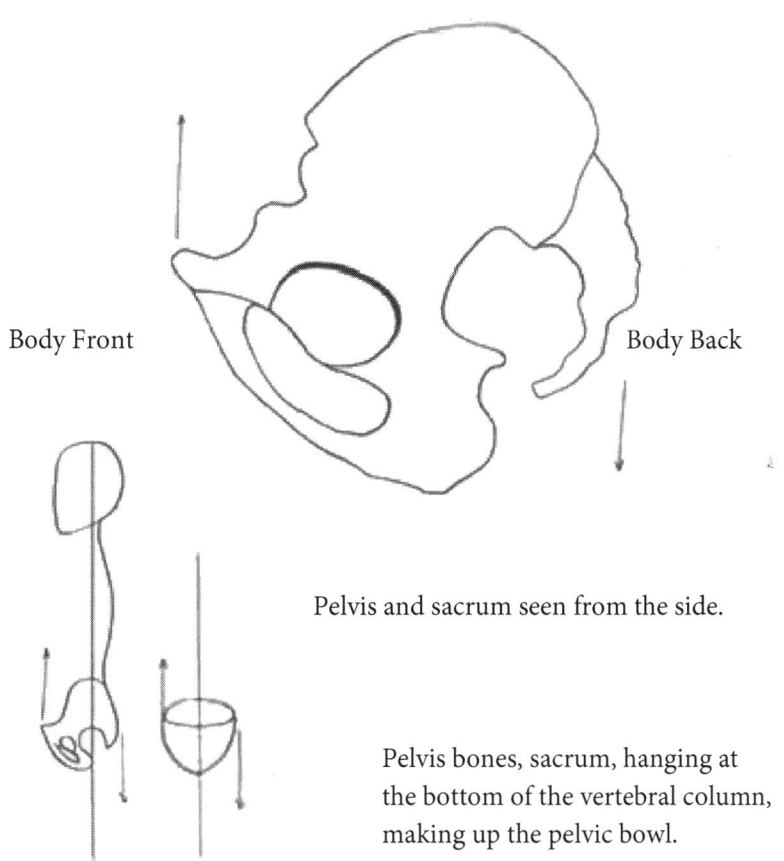

Body Front

Body Back

Pelvis and sacrum seen from the side.

Pelvis bones, sacrum, hanging at the bottom of the vertebral column, making up the pelvic bowl.

The Sacrum and Sternum

The sacrum moves down at the back of the pelvis. The front of the pelvis rises. The vertical abdominal muscles support upwards along the front of the torso and the sternum continues that upward action in the chest, between the ribs.

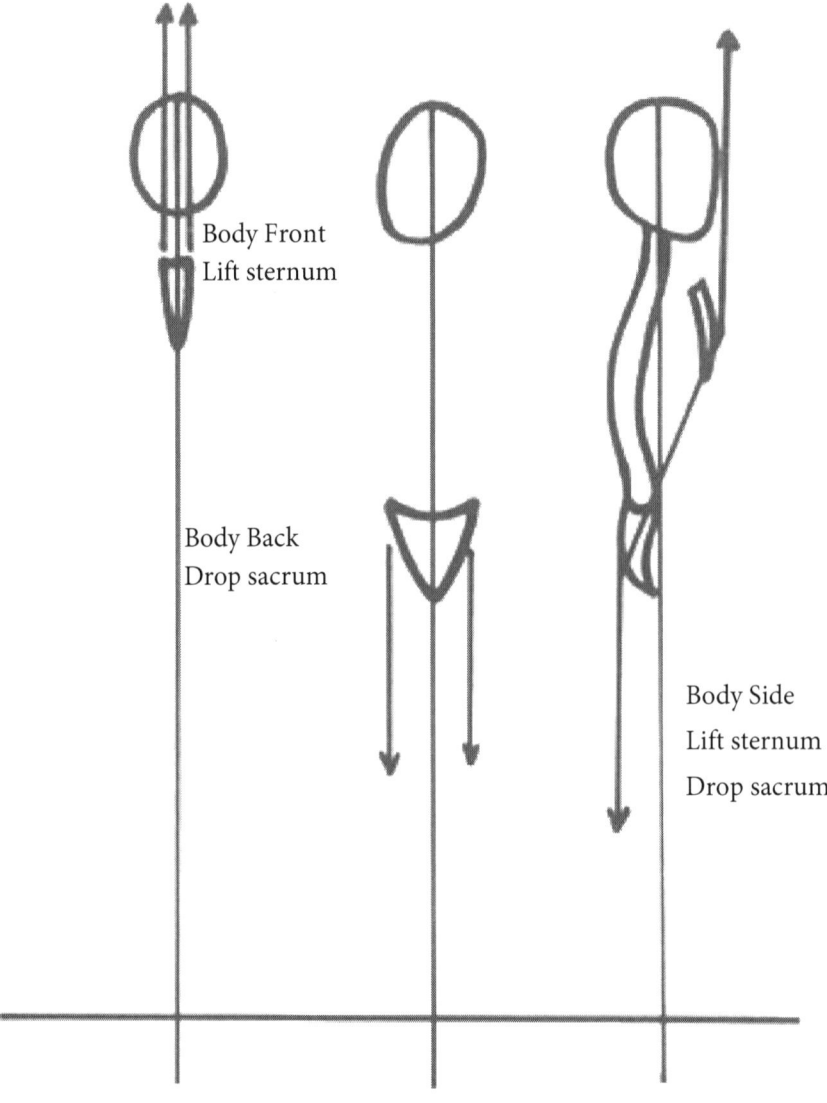

Body Front
Lift sternum

Body Back
Drop sacrum

Body Side
Lift sternum
Drop sacrum

Legs, Arms, Feet and Hands

As weight passes down the back of the leg, the heel drops and the arch of the foot rises. Weight passes up the front of the leg, supporting the knee. As weight passes down the back of the arm, the heel of the hand drops and the arch of the hand rises. Weight passing up the front of the arm supports the elbow.

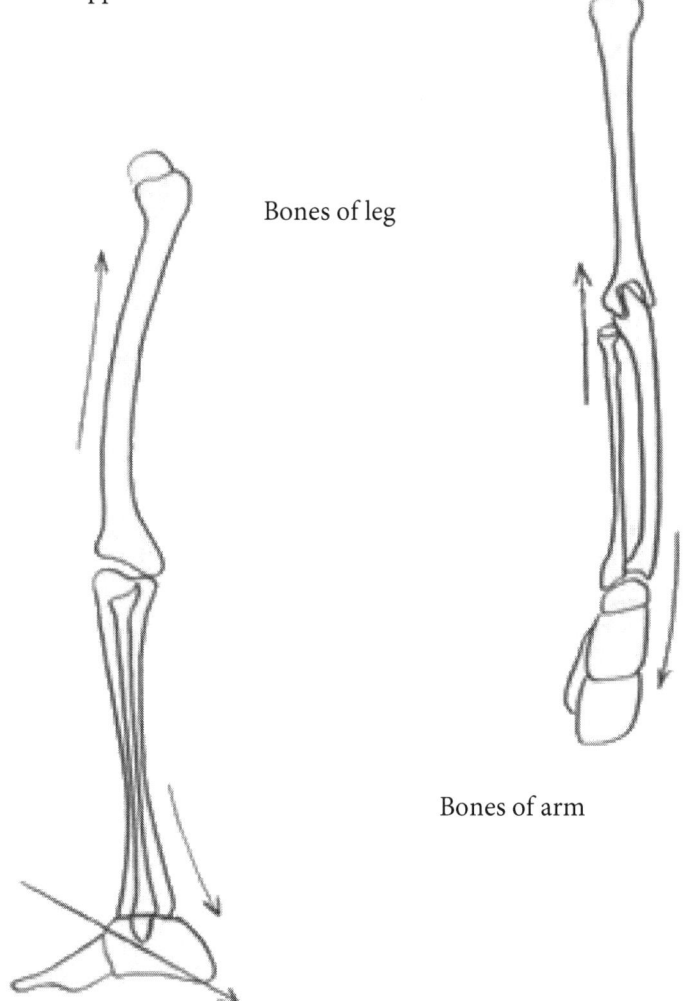

Bones of leg

Bones of arm

Line of action for foot

Heels of Hand and Foot

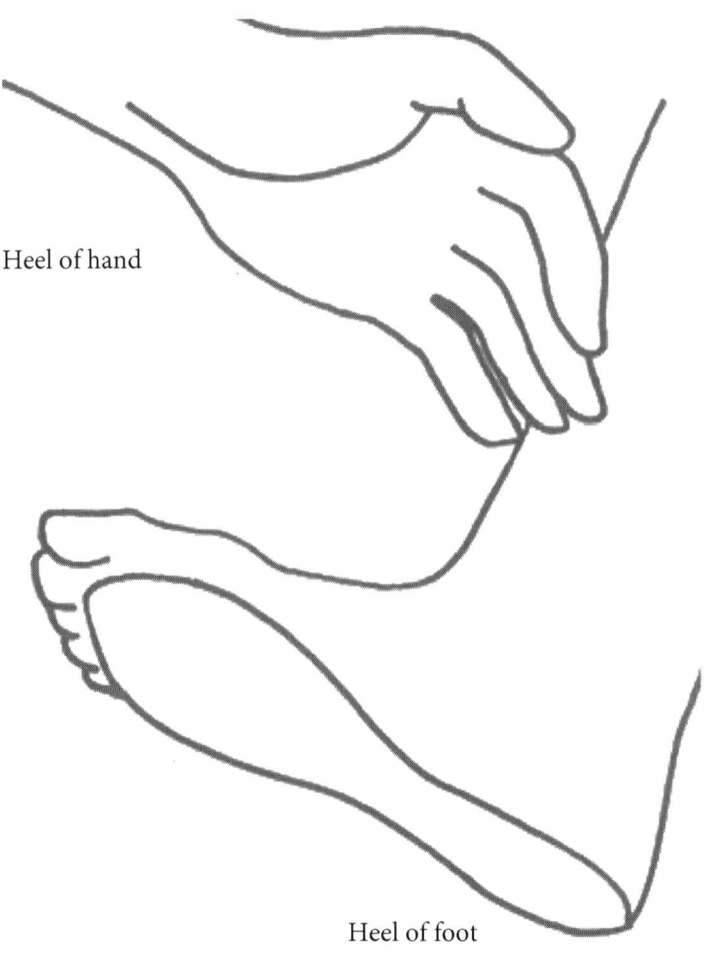

The Face

The face falls deep into the centre of the head. Sensation moves inward and outward at the same time. More than a mask on the front of the head. The face has depth, is the outward receiving part of an entire dialogue between the interior and the world, between perception and action.

UP THE BACK; DOWN THE FACE

The Head

At the top of the vertebral column, high inside the head at the level of the ears and above the point where it rotates around the axis, the head rocks forward and back. The base of the skull rests on two curved surfaces which allow the action of rocking front and back. The second bone from the top, the axis, has a projection which fits up vertically inside the top vertebra, the atlas. Here, between the atlas and the axis, the rotation occurs.

   Rock the head forward and back above the point at which the head turns from side to side.

   Rock the skull on the superior articular facets of the atlas. Rotate between the atlas and the axis.

   Action flows up the back of the head and down the face. Action passes through the place where the head rests on the top vertebra.

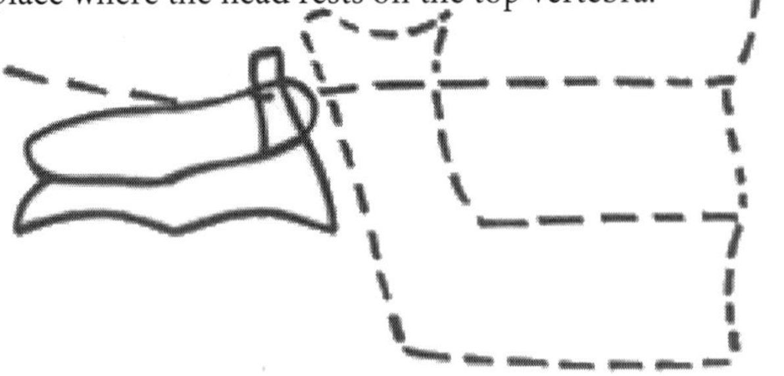

Atlas
and
axis

UP THE BACK AND DOWN THE FACE COMBINED WITH DOWN THE BACK AND UP THE FRONT

Head and Body Head and Arm

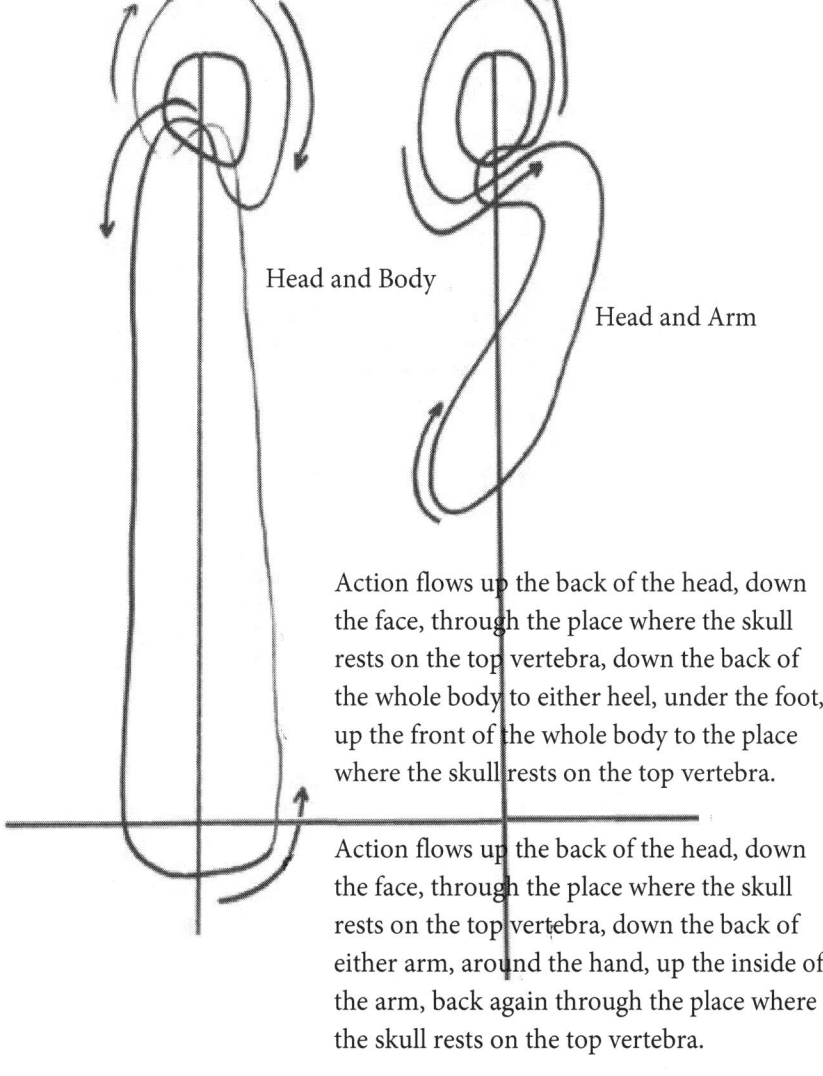

Head and Body

Head and Arm

Action flows up the back of the head, down the face, through the place where the skull rests on the top vertebra, down the back of the whole body to either heel, under the foot, up the front of the whole body to the place where the skull rests on the top vertebra.

Action flows up the back of the head, down the face, through the place where the skull rests on the top vertebra, down the back of either arm, around the hand, up the inside of the arm, back again through the place where the skull rests on the top vertebra.

Body Thinking

The left arm speaks to the right leg through the axis. The right hand knows the left hand through the axis. The head listens to the feet through the axis.

Concentration on a body image can bring to conscious attention a part of thought which ordinarily occurs at an unconscious level. This has the effect of bringing forth an ability to penetrate the barrier between conscious and unconscious thought. A day dream has the full presence of a night dream. Deep feeling can pour outward, even surprising the body with unusual perceptions. One discovers continually that things are not as they seem.

The language of the body can be found below the language of words. Deep feeling, clear perception, the centre of an idea, all these happen underneath words on a sensory level of experience. The world we call real is only a fragment of the whole world. Tremendous participation is possible between a body and a thought. The happenings underneath words can speak directly to anyone who patiently listens.

How to Prepare an Image

Initially, the physical experience of the bones of the body will differ from the objective study of those bones. As one learns to see in such a way that the object seen becomes part of the observer, then thinking about any image becomes simultaneous with the full experience of that image.

Only a small part of possible experience will be found in each initial encounter with an image. Full understanding takes years of patient listening to the messages in the body. Any realisation will be another part of an enormous whole.

Objective study verifies the practical work, but in advanced work the verification is part of the experience of each image. There is, then, no separation between thought and practice. Look at a skeleton or at pictures of the inside of the body.

Look within the body for the experience of study.

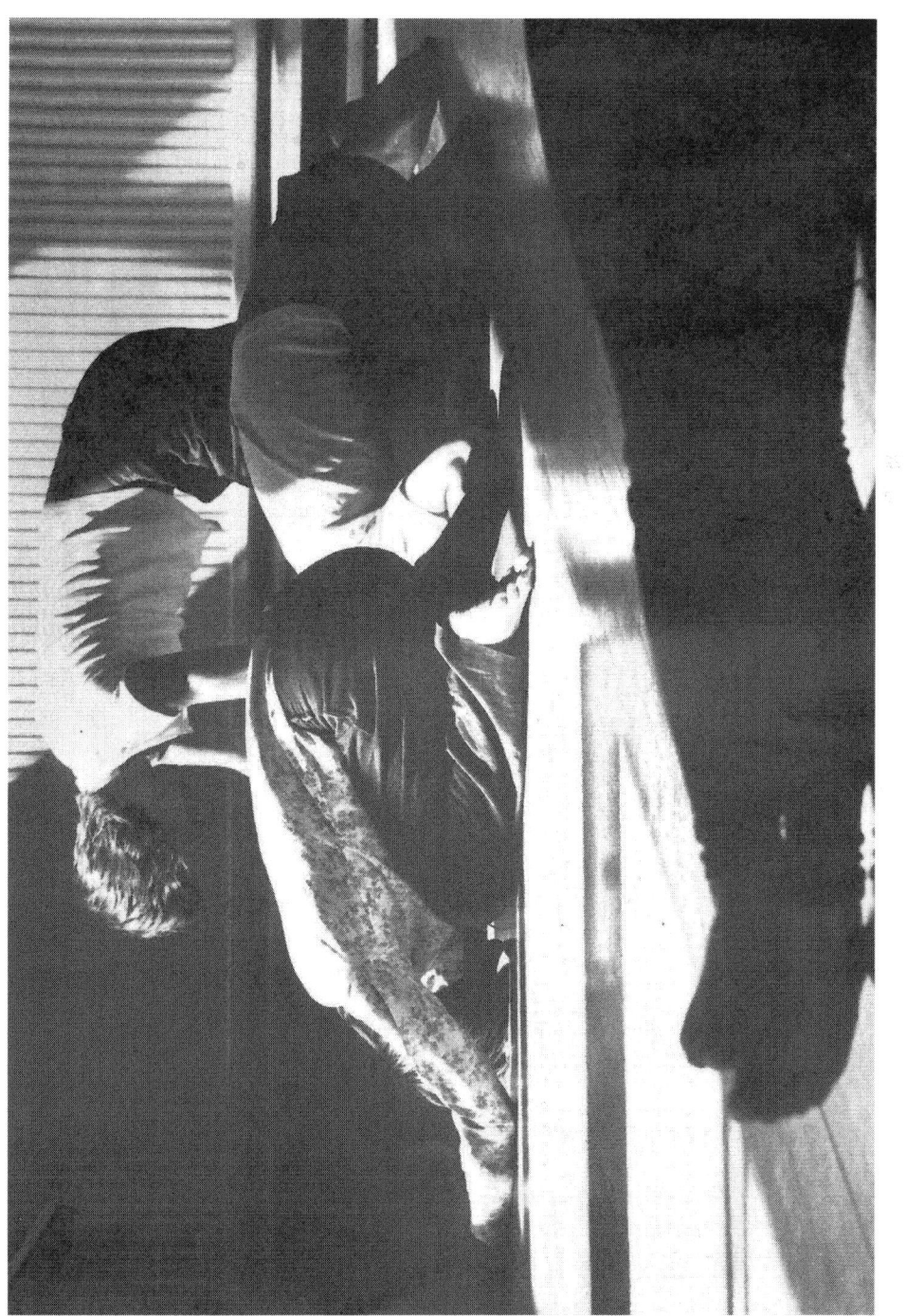

ACTION FLOWS DOWN THE OUTSIDE; UP THE INSIDE

Knees and Legs

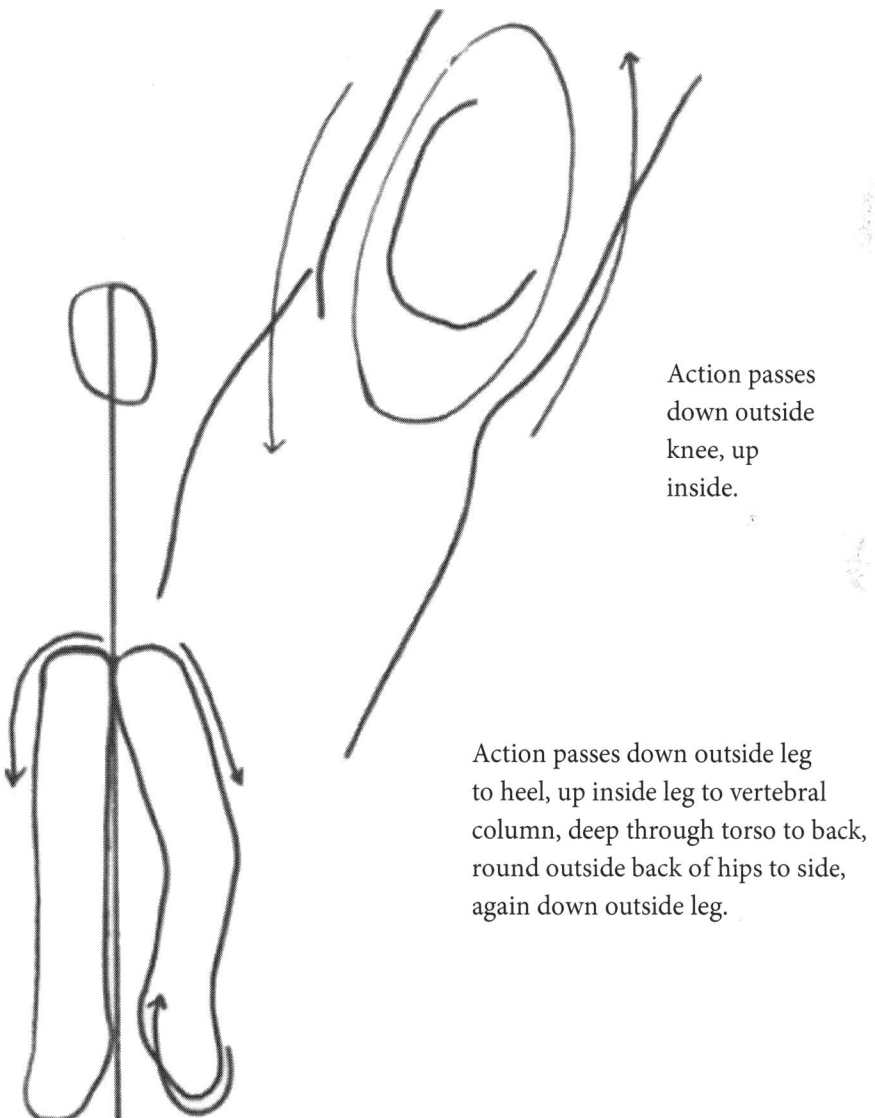

Action passes down outside knee, up inside.

Action passes down outside leg to heel, up inside leg to vertebral column, deep through torso to back, round outside back of hips to side, again down outside leg.

Leg and Foot

Down outside leg to small toe, round front foot to large toe, back again, same direction, to reach centre of arch. Up inside arch, up inside whole leg to vertebral column. Through body to back, round to outside of leg. Repeat both sides.

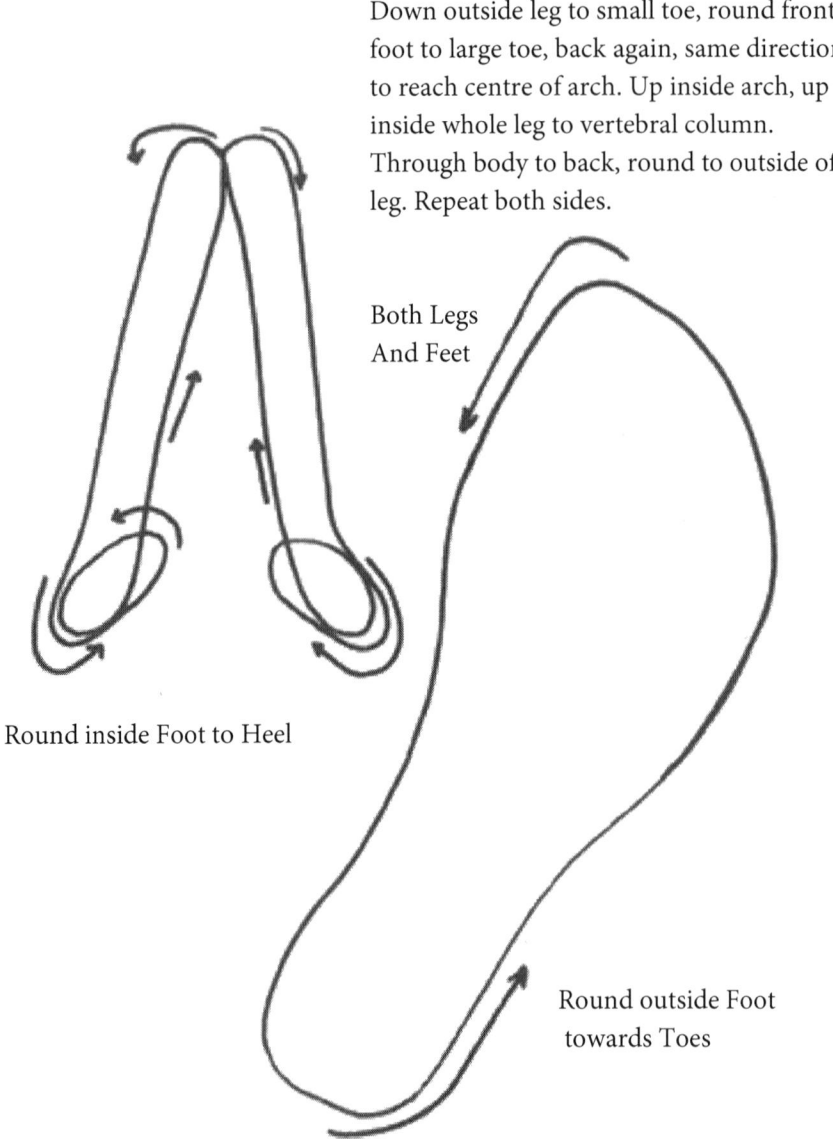

Both Legs And Feet

Round inside Foot to Heel

Round outside Foot towards Toes

Arm and Torso

Down outside arm, up inside. Down outside arm to small finger, up inside, down back to base of vertebral column, through torso to front, upfront, open to shoulder.

One arm, torso, head

Two arms, torso, head

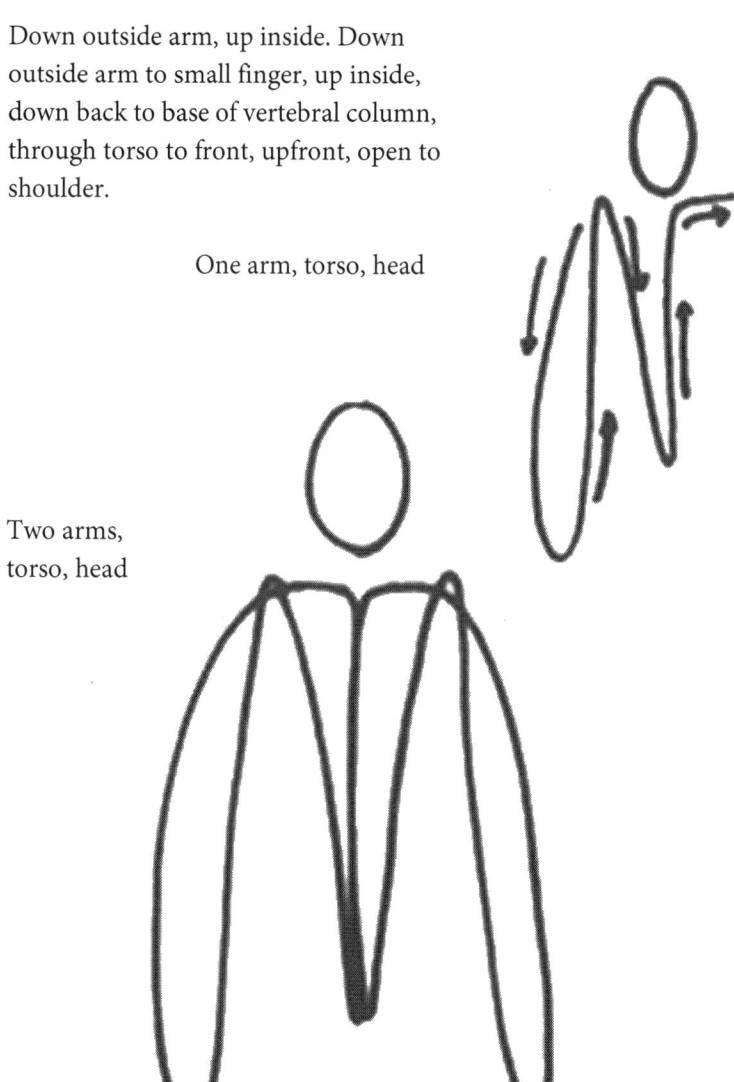

Elbow, Lower Arm and Hand

Down outside elbow, up inside. Down outside elbow to small finger, up inside arm from thumb.

Folding action at elbow brings lower arm into contact with upper arm within a small area at the elbow.

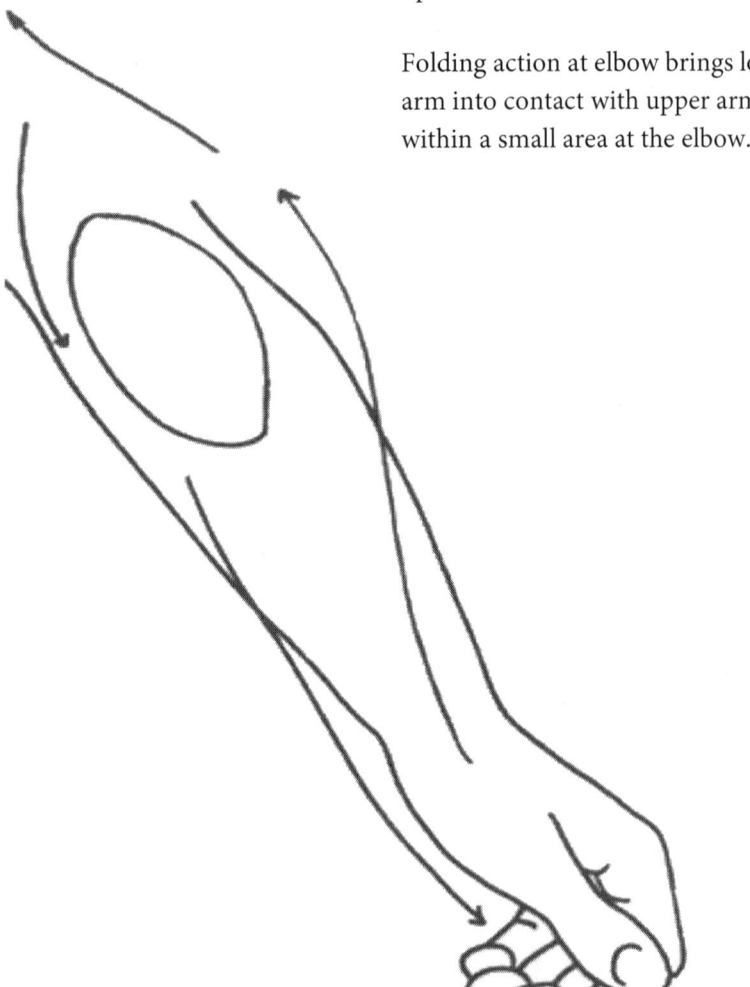

Lower Arm and Lower Leg

Down outside, up inside of lower arm and lower leg.

Hands

Down outside, up inside of hand.

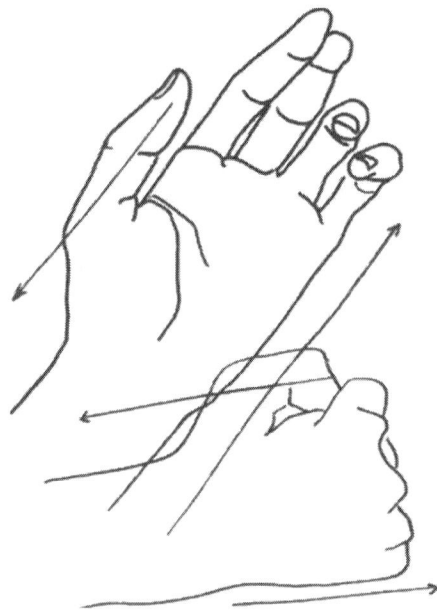

Down outside up inside arms and legs two images superimposed

Action passes down the outside of the arm, up the inside, down the back to the base of the vertebral column, deep through to the front of the torso, up the front, open at the shoulder, and repeat on the other side.

See the images separately, then see them both at the same time.

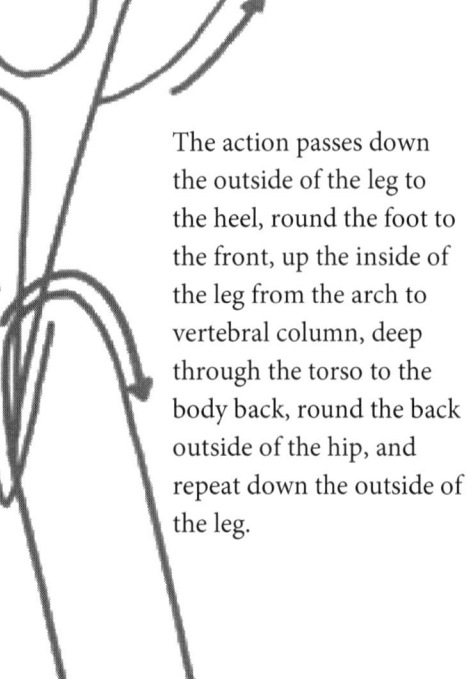

The action passes down the outside of the leg to the heel, round the foot to the front, up the inside of the leg from the arch to vertebral column, deep through the torso to the body back, round the back outside of the hip, and repeat down the outside of the leg.

Down outside up inside same arm and leg working together

When the same arm and leg work together the opposition can occur in the opposite hip. Left arm, right hip, left leg The hip provides stability.

Down outside arm, up inside, down back to base of vertebral column, round outside opposite hip to centre front, deep through torso to back, down back same leg as arm, round foot, up inside leg to vertebral column, up front, open at shoulder and repeat starting on the other side of the body.

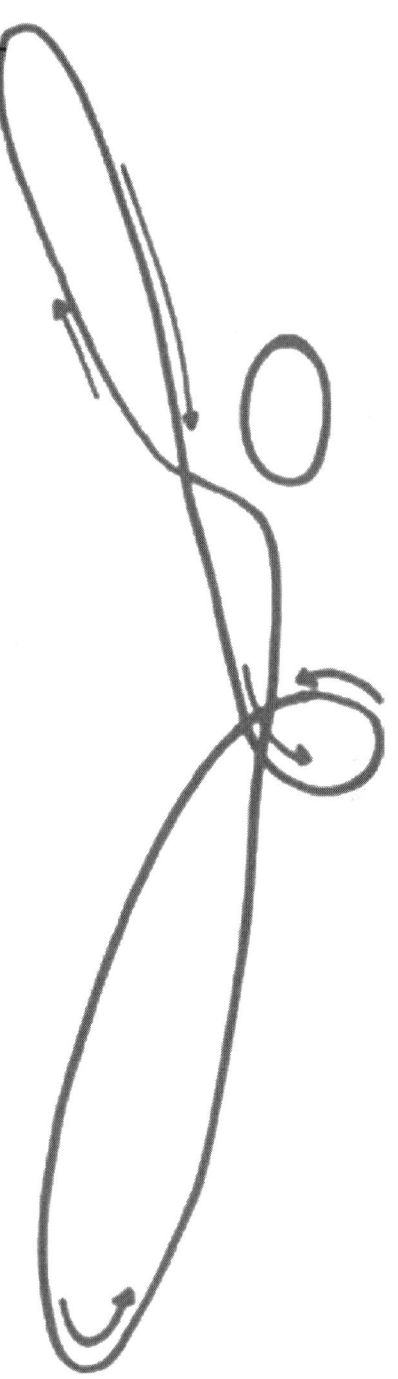

Combined image, arms and legs, down outside, up inside

Down outside arm, up inside, down back to base of vertebral column, down back of opposite leg to heel, round foot to front, to arch, up inside leg from arch, to vertebral column, upfront torso, open at shoulder, and repeat on the other arm and leg.

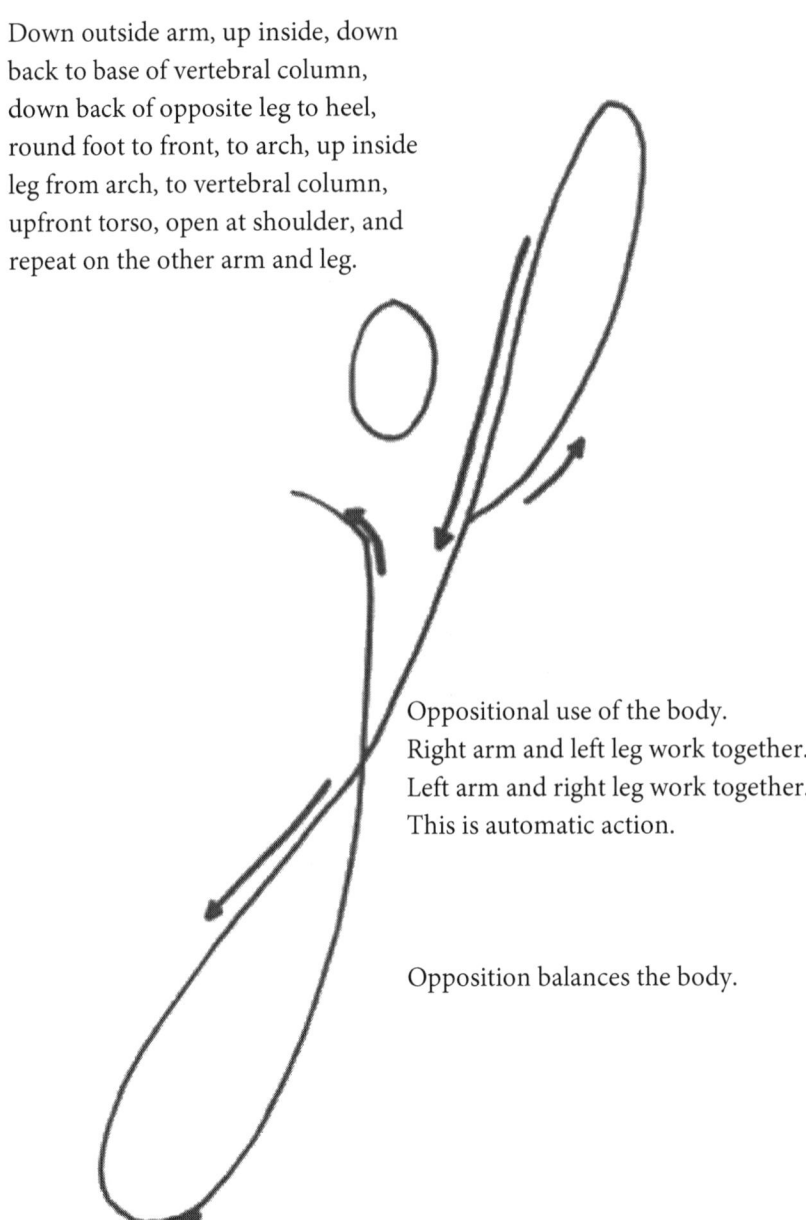

Oppositional use of the body.
Right arm and left leg work together.
Left arm and right leg work together.
This is automatic action.

Opposition balances the body.

Down outside, up inside, arms and legs, image combined, image drawn for both sides of the body.

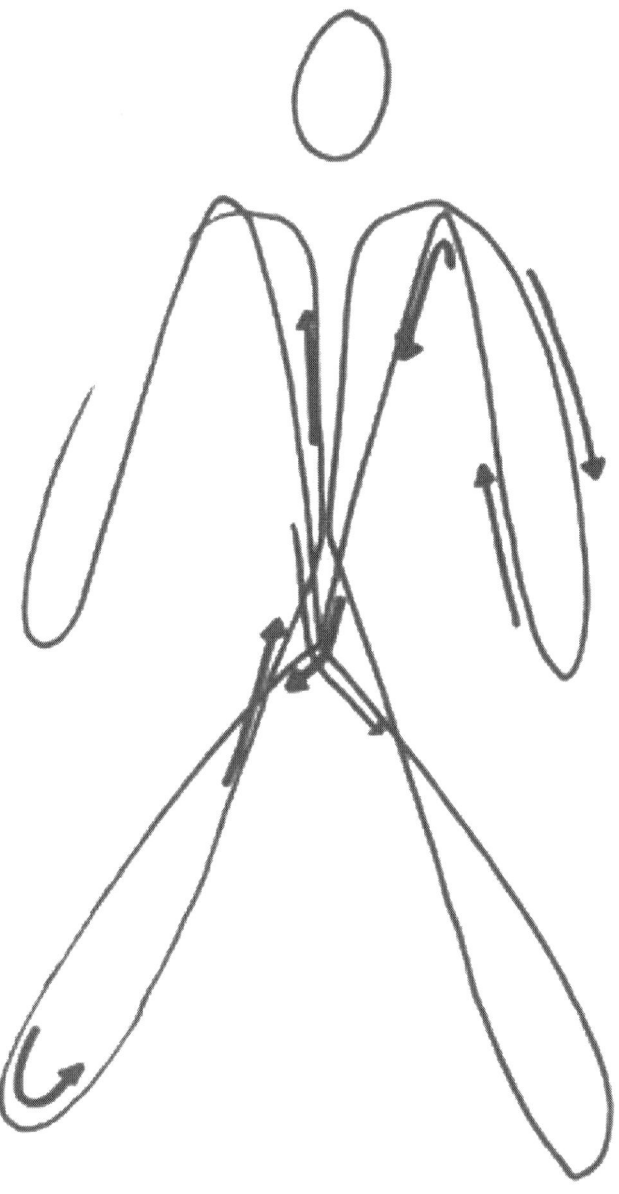

All that the body does is done is determined by the way in which it has habitually functioned. This habitual functioning takes place unconsciously. So, if change is to occur within the body, habitual body movements must change. To make the body stand up straight – whatever that means relative to social and cultural ideas which are rarely based upon the body's anatomy – does little more than affect the body for that moment. As soon as the mind strays from that thought the body re-affirms its usual habits. To cause lasting and permanent change in the body one must let the body receive a message that sinks into the habitual movement process. This cannot be done immediately. It happens after clear intellectual comprehension, after a struggle to allow the image to penetrate movement habits.

The Nature of the Struggle

The body does not accept force well. Habit is a comfortable thing. Where is the struggle?

The mind first struggles to achieve comprehension. Understanding follows later. This is a struggle that is easily recognised. It is like the struggle to comprehend the meaning of a literary allusion. The understanding of the meaning of the allusion goes deeper than the comprehension. With comprehension the allusion becomes clear, useful. With understanding, the allusion becomes forceful, has meaning, has the power to affect sensation in the body and cause feeling changes. Long after the mind comprehends a body image, when the image is an easy companion, then the body understands the image. Only then can the image affect the body's habits.

Changes in the body's habits can occur when a physical sensation is altered repeatedly. One person can give a physical experience to another. Physical experiences such as touching and supporting weight transfer easily between people are understood physically. Such experiences can enter sensation directly. Deep thinking can become the tool that causes change in one's own sensation, in one's own physical experience.

Any physical sensation is not communicated exactly by the words describing that action. But the descriptive words – the verbal image – can be the beginning of the total sensation that it is possible to create by using imaginative thought. It is possible to create sensation from images. It is possible to affect habitual thought with remembered and practiced sensation.

So, one struggles to find a way to allow the body to change its habits. This involves, in the first place, an ability to control and affect sensation through the use of imaginative thought.

ACTION FLOWS ROUND THE OUTSIDE TO FRONT; THROUGH THE CENTRE TO BODY BACK

Shoulders, Hips and Feet

The back widens and the front of the torso supports. Starting at the centre back of the body, action flows round the outside to the front, then directly back through the centre of the body to centre back. This makes one half circle. Repetition on the other side completes the circle. This flow of action in the body takes supporting emphasis off the external muscles of the back and shares the supporting function with the front body wall. As a result, weight is carried through bones of the vertebral column deep in the centre of the body.

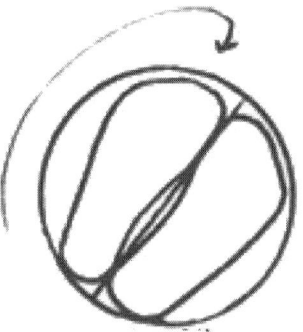

Standing in a Circle

Action flows round the outside of the foot towards the toes, back to the heel passing the arch. This flow of action follows ideal weight transfer from heel to toes in normal walking. As the line from heel to small toe becomes longer, the arch lifts.

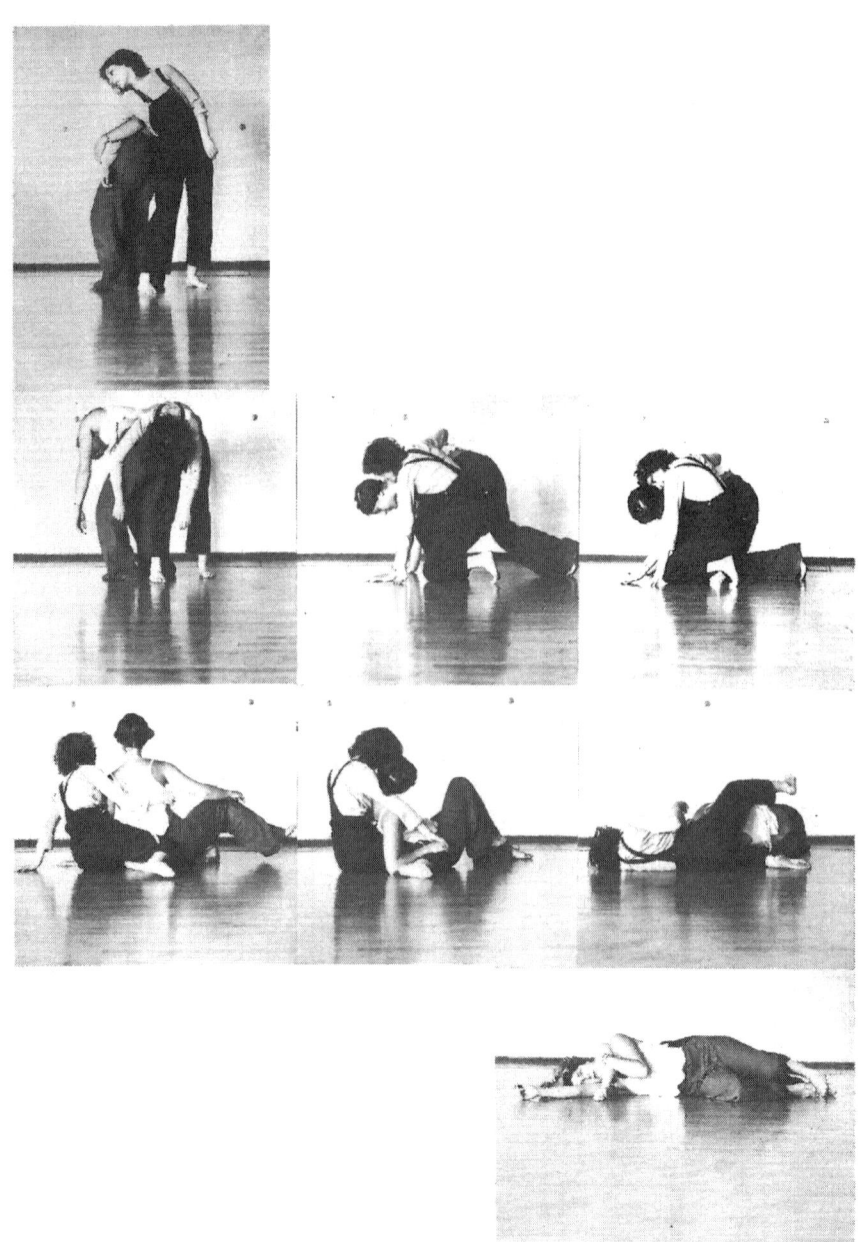

Round the outside through the centre, shoulders and hips

Right shoulder, left hip. Opposition, shoulder and hip. Round outside shoulder to front, through centre to back, down back, at hip level, round hip to front, up torso front, deep through torso at shoulder level arriving at back. Repeat using other shoulder and hip.

Right shoulder, right hip. Same shoulder and hip. Round back and outside of shoulder to front, deep through torso to back, down back to hip level, round same hip as shoulder, to front, up front torso to shoulder level, deep through torso at shoulder level to back. Repeat using other shoulder and hip.

Round outside through centre to back of ribs

(Round outside; up in front of body parallel to central vertical axis - an image for the ribs)

Circle each rib round outside to front, then let action lift in front – a line parallel to the centre line, several inches in front of the centre line. Again the image supports the body up the front, taking weight off the superficial muscles of the back and sharing weight throughout the torso.

Circle each rib from back to front, through body centre to back. Both sides. Twelve circles on each side.

Round the outside, back through centre, shoulder, opposite hip, opposite foot, combined with up the front, down the back of torso and legs

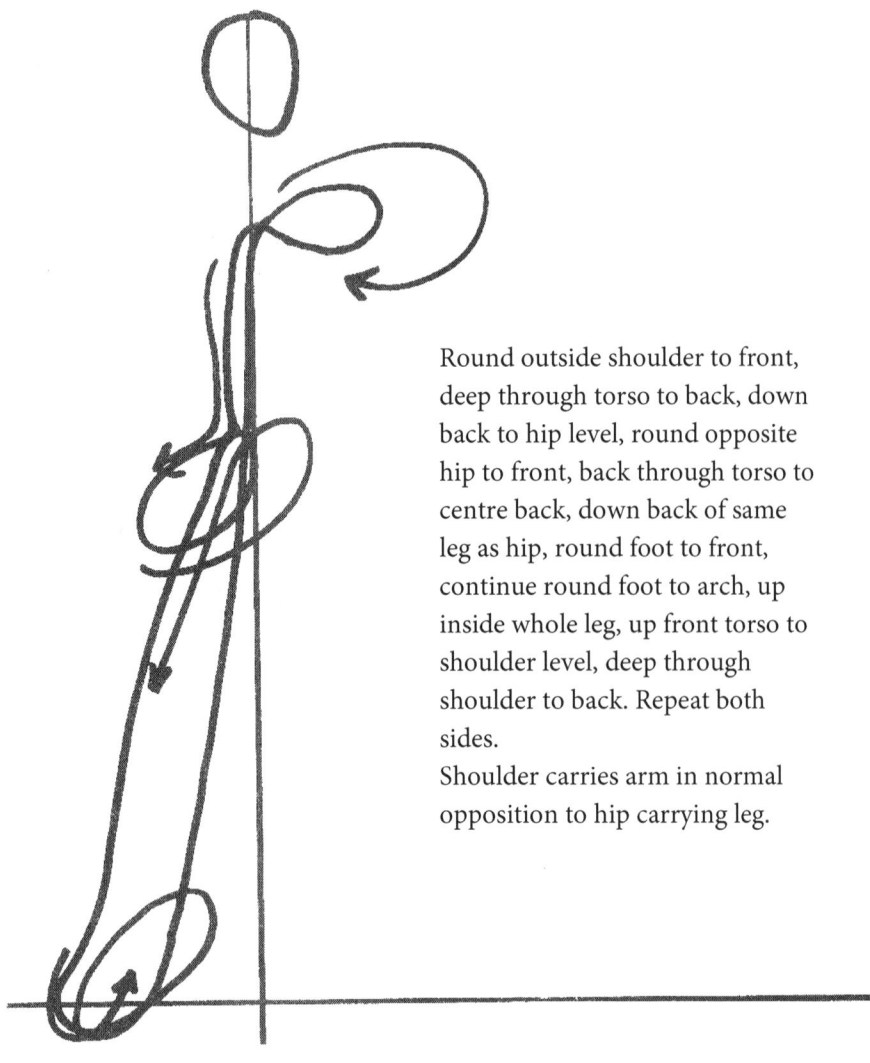

Round outside shoulder to front, deep through torso to back, down back to hip level, round opposite hip to front, back through torso to centre back, down back of same leg as hip, round foot to front, continue round foot to arch, up inside whole leg, up front torso to shoulder level, deep through shoulder to back. Repeat both sides.
Shoulder carries arm in normal opposition to hip carrying leg.

Round the outside, back through centre, shoulder, opposite hip, same foot, combined with up the front, down the back of torso and legs

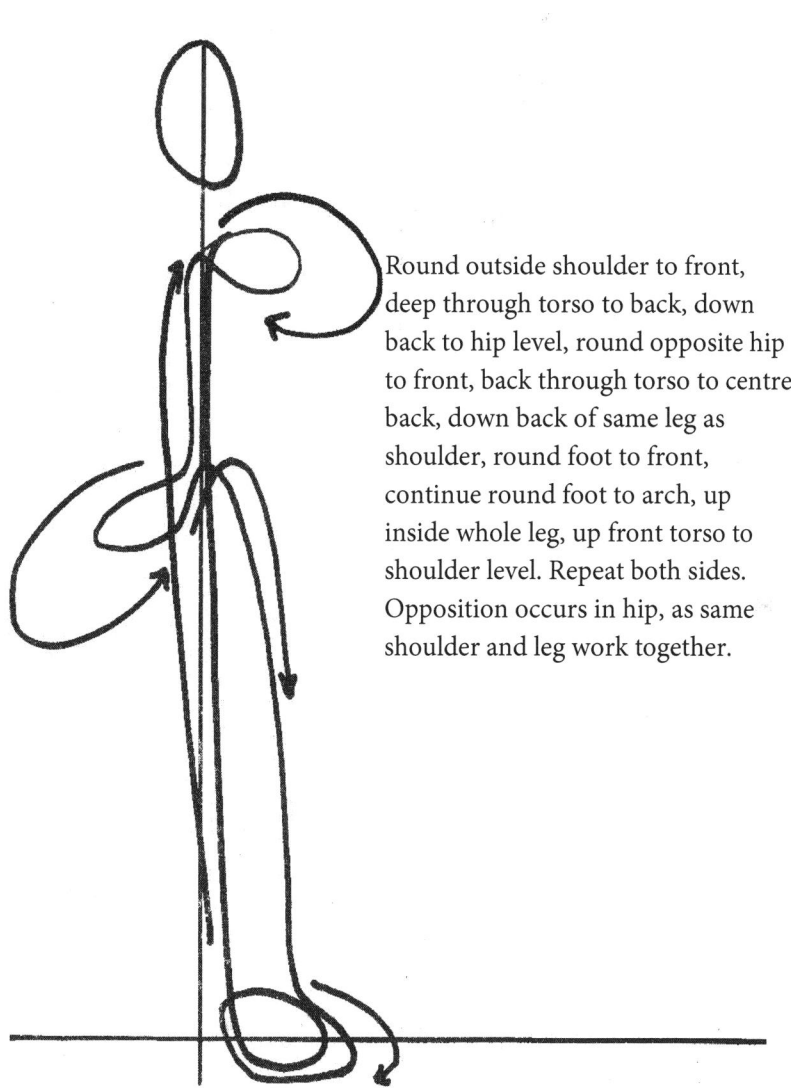

Round outside shoulder to front, deep through torso to back, down back to hip level, round opposite hip to front, back through torso to centre back, down back of same leg as shoulder, round foot to front, continue round foot to arch, up inside whole leg, up front torso to shoulder level. Repeat both sides. Opposition occurs in hip, as same shoulder and leg work together.

Round the outside, back through centre, images seen separately, and with, up the back, down the face

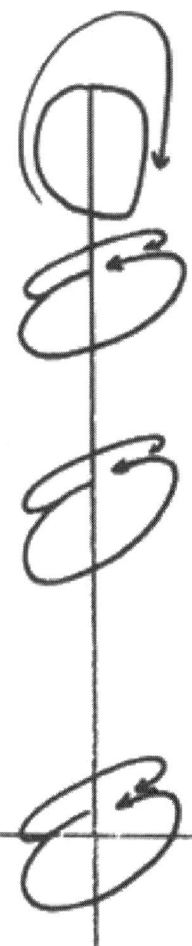

Action flows up the back of the head, down the face, making a circle. This flow of action lengthens supporting muscles in the back of the neck so the head finds an easy balance on top of the vertebral column.

Passing on to the shoulder level, one image becomes part of a larger context when combined with others. At the shoulder level action flows round the outside of the body to the front, back through centre to the back.

At hip level action flows round the outside to the front, through centre to the back.

And consider the image for the feet, stand in a circle.

Round the outside through the centre combined with up the back down the face and down the back of the torso and legs, up the front.

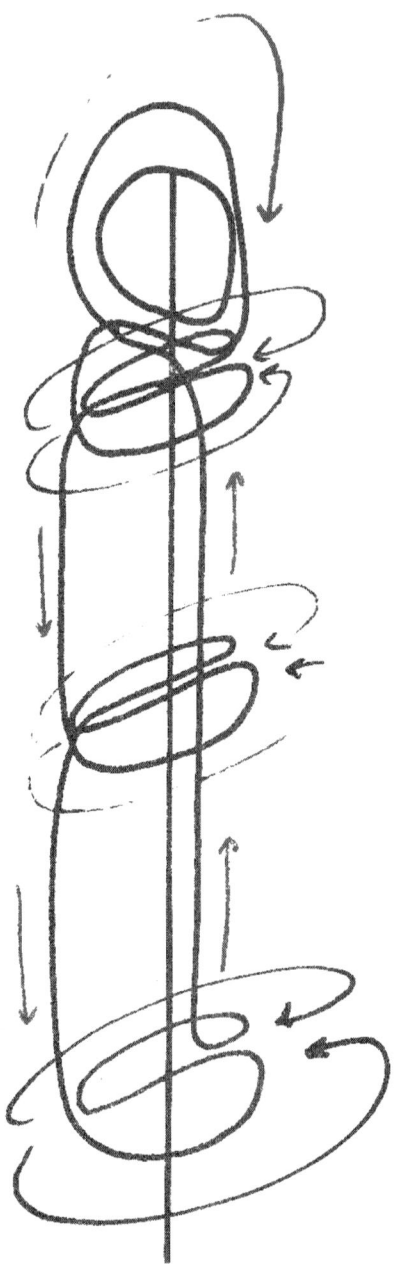

Action flows up the back of the head, down the face, through the place where the head rests on the vertebral column, down the back to shoulder level, round the outside of the shoulder to the front, back through centre, round the opposite shoulder to the front, back through centre completing shoulder circle, down back to hip level. Round outside hip to front, back through centre, round opposite hip completing circle and down back to one heel. Round foot to front, back through centre, round opposite foot to front, back to centre, completing circle. From arch of one foot draw action upward in front of leg, in front of torso, to place where head rests on vertebral column. This whole image repeats on the other side of the body, circling first to the other side, and using the opposite arch to begin action upward. With repetition on the opposite side the image becomes entirely symmetrical. A continuous flow of action through all three images as they are combined will give a total body harmony.

PART TWO: EASY ACTION

In working it is useful to have a group of very easy actions which can accompany any developing movement thought. A few simple actions are suggested here. These possibilities are easily held in the memory, ready for when the body demands them, not before. One must stop directing the body and start listening to interior suggestion. Look for gracious listening.

Every easy action can be used to practise every body image. Some correlations will be more obvious at first, but eventually a total inter-change becomes possible.

REST POSITION

Whole weight is given to floor surface.

Lying on side of body, head rests easily on one arm which is folded. Other arm rests along top side of body, slightly folded at elbow, hand on hip. Knees are at right angles to hips, lower legs at right angles to thighs. One foot rests comfortably over the other. Back of torso is long. Head is a continuation of back length. Support may be used under head.

Or, lying on back of body, arms rest easily below shoulder level. Knees are bent, feet flat on floor. Head rests in the central axis of the torso. Weight of thighs falls into torso. Back is long, falling onto the surface of the floor. Knees may rest together, supporting each other, but this should be unnecessary. Legs ought to balance easily. Head may be raised slightly by a firm support. Alternatively both arms may rest across front of chest.

STILLNESS

Resting in either rest position, or standing, find the possibility of listening to the body. Experience the inner complexity. Breath is easy. Weight is allowed to fall -given to the floor surface. Develop the quality of patience. In stillness, waiting is not necessary. Stillness is a positive state, complete and full in its expression. Do not wait for the end of stillness. Stillness is not an absence or expectation of movement. It is stillness.

Stillness comes in many shapes.

ROLL

Easily turn the weight of the body along the surface of the floor. Use hands and feet. Let legs rise up toward torso and roll onto knees or onto back with legs lifted. Legs fold and lengthen easily in rolling. Knees are soft, bending easily, ready to take weight. Body turns, all parts falling to floor surface, even head. Whole body gently rolling. The twist which begins rolling may originate in many places throughout the body. Rotation comes at the axis of motion which is at the centre of the body. Foot aids function of lower leg. Side and top of foot are useful in rolling. Look for easy ways to roll. The body knows.

ROLL TO SIT

Roll around a central axis. Bring legs toward torso. Find leverage in hip articulation and roll up the side of the body, using hands to support action if necessary. Turn up to sit easily with a long back, balanced.

Sitting takes place through the whole torso and the legs are free to move below. Sit balanced evenly on the bony supports at the base of the torso. Sit like a baby.

Return to rolling using leverage at hips, supporting body through the centre, using hands and arms as needed.

Roll and return to sit.

Repetition is important. Intellectual knowing precedes the physical understanding.

ROLL TO CRAWL

Rolling easily along the surface of the floor, let knees and elbows bend and fold into the torso. Roll onto arms and legs, making the shape of a small round ball. Supported by hands and knees, unfold torso to crawl. Arms and thighs are perpendicular to floor. Feet rest behind with insteps on surface of floor. Ankles may fall to outside letting toes of both feet pass near each other in the action of crawling on hands and knees. Arms and legs swing from high inside the body. Each limb appears to move alone and an easy action is achieved which feels very

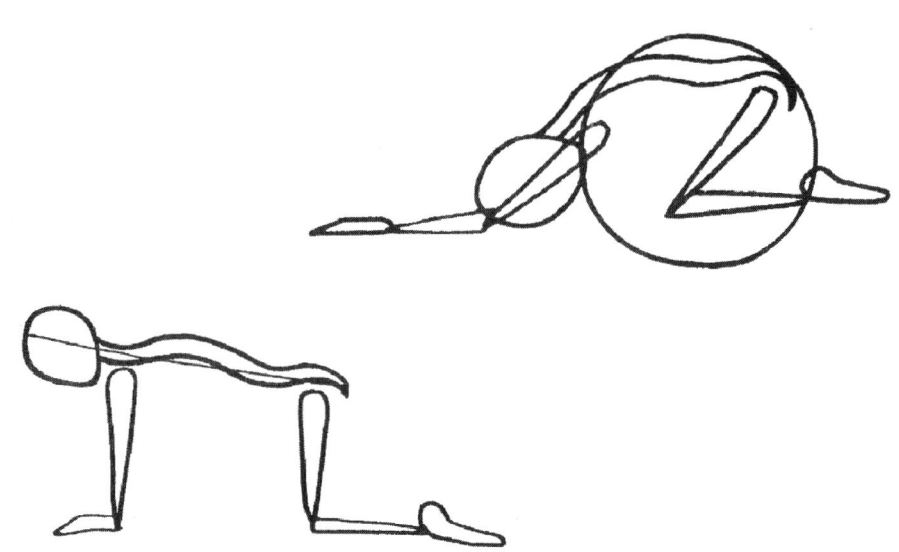

much like walking. The back is actually not parallel to the floor, due to the fact that arms are longer than thighs. Torso is a long line. Back is wide and flat.

Length in torso remains constant as arms and legs swing to crawl. Head is a continuation of torso, back of neck very long. Hands and feet are used parallel to each other, or slightly turned in at fingers and toes. Shoulder blades are included with surface of back as broad and wide as possible. Whole body seeks harmony. Easy action comes from leverage which is physically understood. Crawl forward and backward. Return to roll. Crawl again. Easy alternation between rolling and crawling.

ROLL TO STAND

Roll with a central axis. Fold arms and legs into torso to arrive at the small ball shape preceding crawling. Pass through crawling to put weight on hands and feet. Let head hang heavily toward floor as whole body is supported over hands and feet. Walk hands back toward feet, letting hips rise slightly. Weight falls to legs, freeing arms which continue to hang down. Knees are bent. Begin to uncurve bottom of back with head and arms still hanging. Knees lengthen as back uncurves. Arrive standing; head is the last body part to fall into the central vertical axis. Body is long, soft support at knees and ankles; float around a central vertical axis.

Or, easily turning along the surface of the floor, find leverage that comes from opening folded hips and legs. Let that leverage continue as whole body rolls, uncurves, and lengthens to stand. Rely on the momentum of the rolling which causes whole body to stand easily. Rolling becomes turning and uncurving to stand. Use hands for support as needed This is the same back and head action as before, but done as the body is turning to vertical.

Or, easily turning along the surface of the floor, find leverage that comes from opening folded hips and legs. Let that leverage continue as whole body rolls, uncurves and lengthens to stand. Rely on the momentum of the rolling which causes whole body to stand easily. Rolling becomes turning and uncurving to stand. Use hands for support as needed. This is the same back and head action as before, but done as the body is turning to vertical.

STAND; CURVE FORWARD; UNCURVE

Standing balanced around a central vertical axis, let weight of head move forward and down. Top of head curves forward first. Action continues down back of torso until upper body is curved far forward over supporting legs. Knees slide easily forward to deepen and widen back curve and to deepen folding action in hips. Uncurving, lower back lengthens up first. Action continues until whole body comes to balance around central vertical axis. It is important that action continues through whole length of torso. Arms slide easily forward as body curves, and then slide easily back as body lengthens to stand upright. Knees fold straight forward, maintaining same distance from each other throughout back curve and uncurve. Knees slide forward and back. Feet remain parallel throughout. Curve head and uncurve bottom of back first. Keep the flow of action continuous. Thoughtful action continues in standing stillness between repetitions.

STAND TO CRAWL

Stand with a central vertical axis. Curve forward. When torso is folded completely forward, over legs, hands rest on floor surface, palms down. Knees are very bent. Heels of feet are on floor. Hands take body weight as they walk away from feet. Knees bend easily to meet floor, first one, then the other. Crawl on hands and knees.

Or, turning while curving, momentum carries body easily down and forward into crawl position. Initial action is down and around. Second action is forward onto hands and to crawl position. Both actions flow together.

From crawl to stand, feet prepare to take weight by folding forward at ankles. Balls of feet meet floor surface. Both knees leave floor surface, hips rise, weight rests on hands and feet. Hands walk back to transfer whole weight to bent knees. Body is in extreme forward curve. Uncurve to stand.

KNEES BEND

Stand around a central vertical axis, feet parallel to each other, a few inches apart. Allow torso to remain long, back of body is wide. Let knees slide easily forward, causing folding in hips, knees and ankles. Keep whole foot on floor for the duration of the action. Rest as working. Let knees slide easily back to lengthen throughout whole body. When knees fold they remain the same distance apart as when standing. Length and width of torso remain constant throughout the action. Allow gravity to act on torso, hanging long around a vertical, supporting centre.

Small knee bends may be done in a variety of foot positions. As the hip rotates outward knees will be bending apart from each other and lengthening will bring knees together. When foot position changes, hip, knee, ankle and second toe of foot remain constantly working on the same vertical plane.

There is no useful effect achieved by forcing the action. Forcing merely applies excessive tension which actually inhibits action. Work constructively by experiencing desirable change on a small scale, and then allow change to occur over a period of time; recreate from physical memory the experienced desirable change. The body can change if ideas about how the body moves become clear. Initially this clarity may mean very small, slow, careful movements. All the simple actions described here will function to develop physical memories and in this way act to develop constructive habitual movement.

DEEP KNEE BEND

Heels lift off floor surface only as necessary. Torso remains upright during action. Returning to stand, heels press down against floor surface. This initiates the upward action.

Knees bend with any leg position, while torso and head maintain balance around the vertical axis. There is one line of action from hip to centre of knee to centre of ankle to second toe. This establishes an axis for each leg to work. Knees work in the axis of the leg, ankle works in the axis of leg and foot, foot works in the axis of leg. The axis is decided by the hip. Hip also decides where body may step.

SIT TO CRAWL

Sit around a centre line. Action takes place in hips. Leverage gained in changing position of thighs relative to torso gives easy action. Sit with sides of legs and feet on floor in the following position:

One leg is folded across front of body with whole outside of leg on floor surface. other leg is folded next to body, foot behind, lower leg outside thigh, and whole inside of leg on floor surface.

Change the axis of torso by rocking slightly forward and pushing legs behind torso to crawl position. Weight is taken on both hands as torso shifts forward.

Rocking torso forward sends legs to back. Hips rise as torso is rocked forward. That leads to easy action into crawl position. Once proper leverage is achieved, this change becomes very comfortable. Back remains broad and long throughout action if initial movement of axis is taken with whole torso providing leverage.

CRAWL ON HANDS AND FEET

Crawl on hands and feel. Weight remains between hands and feet, not balanced forward or behind. Arms swing easily from shoulders. Legs swing easily from hips. Arms and legs alternate in action, crawling forward or backward. Head rests as part of torso, top of head hanging toward floor. Action for legs begins high in torso front. Action for arms finds leverage throughout the length of back. Arms and legs bend easily at elbows and knees.

SQUAT

Stand around a central vertical axis. Curve forward, head beginning curve, and at the same time fold at hips, knees and ankles. Sit all the way down to squat with both knees folded against chest and both heels on floor. Torso is a long forward curve supported above feet.

Arms reach forward to balance body. Knees remain as far apart as they were at the start of action. Arches of feet remain lifted throughout action, and both feet stay parallel.

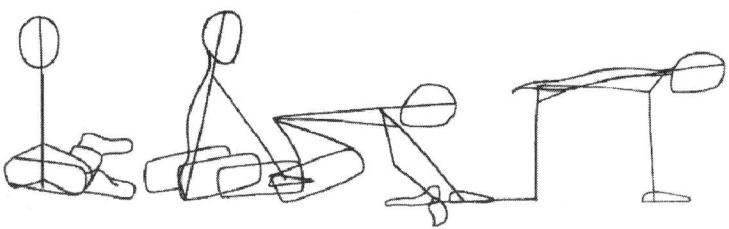

DOUBLE SQUAT

If the squat is difficult at first, it is possible to work in pairs facing each other.

Hold hands. Two people support each other, leaning away from each other and holding hands. Two people squat at the same lime, their weights counterbalancing each other.

CRAWL; SIT BACK ON HEELS; KNEEL

Crawl with a long, broad back. Bring legs and arms perpendicular to the floor. Settle back gently into hips so that back lengthens and curves, and chest rests down on thighs. Arrive sitting on heels, curved forward. Let bottom of torso maintain contact with heels and slowly uncurve from bottom of back first so back becomes vertical and at last head, too, is in the same centre line – sitting on heels. Next, find leverage from hips and torso, to rock whole torso forward and upward to kneel. Head, torso, thighs, and knees are in the same vertical line. Balance easily whilst kneeling.

Again shift whole axis forward and allow one leg to swing forward, sharing support of torso with leg remaining behind. Now head, torso, rear thigh and knee make one line.

Rock backward by pushing with forward leg and return to kneel evenly over both knees. Balance in line, head to knees. Sit down onto heels, rock whole torso forward to crawl, let arms swing forward to catch weight equally on both hands. Crawl position. Repeat, alternating which leg swings forward.

WALK

Stand around a central vertical axis. Whole body falls forward in one piece. One leg swings forward to catch falling body with an easy step. Fall forward again with whole body, swing back leg to front and step again. Walking happens when bodyweight falls and is caught by stepping.

Legs swing high inside hips. Leverage comes from deep and high inside front of torso. Knees bend and straighten easily.

Arms swing easily. Arm action takes place deep inside shoulders. Arms derive leverage from whole back length of torso.

Arms and legs gain leverage from vertebral column which approximates central vertical axis in body. The vertebral column is sometimes called the common lever in the body because all limbs derive leverage from muscles attached to the vertebrae. So, all four limbs have the vertebral column as their lever – they have this in common.

This is also true of the head. The head can be seen as a fifth limb or as part of the vertebral column.

Find that the arm and leg action in walking is related to the vertebral column. Swing arms from back of torso, feeling that leverage comes from full length of back.

Swing legs from the front of torso, feeling that their leverage comes from deep inside the front lower half of torso.

Walking is like crawling. In both of these, action begins by falling forward with the whole central axis, but this is such a small fall that it is not normally perceived. Arms and legs swing in a similar manner in walking and crawling.

Foot pattern when stepping forward is heel first, then through foot to toes. When stepping backwards, toes lead, action crosses through foot to heel.

Each arm swings slightly across front of body. Right arm and left leg work together. Left arm and right leg work together. This is automatic action and is called opposition.

Walk forward and backward. Take steps sending axis to side and recovering balance with feet apart. Then bring feet together. Walk in organised patterns of steps. Front, back, side, side, front, back, back, together. Repeat many times. Make a simple series and become lost in walking.

RUN

Balance around a central vertical axis. Send whole axis falling fast forward. Continue falling until a moderately large step is required to recover balance. Hips, knees and ankles fold more than in walking. Arms are bent slightly at elbows. Hands rise as arms swing forward from high inside shoulders. Arms maintain a forward-backward action, slightly crossing in front of torso as they swing forward. Centre of weight is carried lower in running than in walking.

Head action is simply to rest in line with the axis. Back of neck is long.

Leg action is forward and backward. Arches of feet remain lifted. Knees fold straight forward. Action at hips directs action in legs. Action of foot goes immediately to ball of foot without heel first.

Right arm forward calls left leg forward. Left arm forward calls right leg forward. Right leg forward calls left arm forward. Left leg forward calls right arm forward.

Run for ten minutes.

Run with a partner.

RAISE ARM

Balance around central axis in body, sitting, kneeling or standing. Raise and lower first one arm, then the other. Action begins near central vertical axis. Keep hands close to torso at first. Fingers follow a line in front of the central vertical axis and parallel to it. Lift arm, raise hand above head. Let arm return down by retracing the same line.

Lift arm from action throughout whole back of torso. Let shoulder, elbow and wrist easily fold or lengthen as necessary. To raise arm with hand near torso, fold greatly at shoulder and elbow. To raise arm with hand far from torso fold less at elbow and wrist and take action largely at shoulder.

Back of torso lifts arms. Lifting close to central axis is easier than lifting arm from central axis.

Begin: arms lift close to centre. Continue: arms lift in wide arcs. Maintain easy action of work.

Hands function harmoniously with lower arms. Hands are held softly, ready to take weight or ready to establish contact with any surface.

STILL BALANCE

Stand around a central vertical axis, bodyweight balanced over two parallel feet. Then curve forward until hands rest easily on floor. Knees bend. Un-curve and shift whole axis to side so one foot easily leaves floor. Body weight is balanced over one leg and foot. Central axis remains long through standing leg.

Whole axis falls again to centre. Curve forward. Replace raised foot. Arrive curved forward, body weight balanced evenly on both feet. Vertical centre. Repeat both sides.

Balance happens when body parts fall into line. Balance is not held. It is allowed.

CURVE AND FALL

Stand around a central vertical axis. Weight of head brings torso curving forward. Back stays long and wide throughout curve. Squat. Rest backward out of squat and quickly unfold torso along floor surface, head coming last to rest position. This sitting back to lie down is one rapid, easy action. Often one thigh lifts toward chest balancing action of torso uncurving.

Two ways to return to stand:

Raise both legs up over head, causing curve in torso. Thighs approach chest. Use arms and hands to balance weight over head, neck and shoulders. Hips are raised and supported by arms when legs are back over head. Then lift head forward, and roll up through sitting to squat, all in one large, forward swinging action (Hips roll down as head rolls up). Squat. Uncurve by partially lengthening legs and raising hips. Complete leg lengthening as back uncurves to stand. Head arrives last.

Or, roll whole body onto side. Arms and thighs fold to chest. Hands and feet prepare to take body weight. Roll to crawl, hands and knees. Then crawl hands and feet. Walk hands back to feet. Weight over legs. Uncurve.

Action comes from torso. Front body wall supports lying down and swinging up actions. Back body wall supports curve forward. Leverage in hips becomes important to maintain easy action, especially through squat to rest on back and again in swing and roll back up to stand.

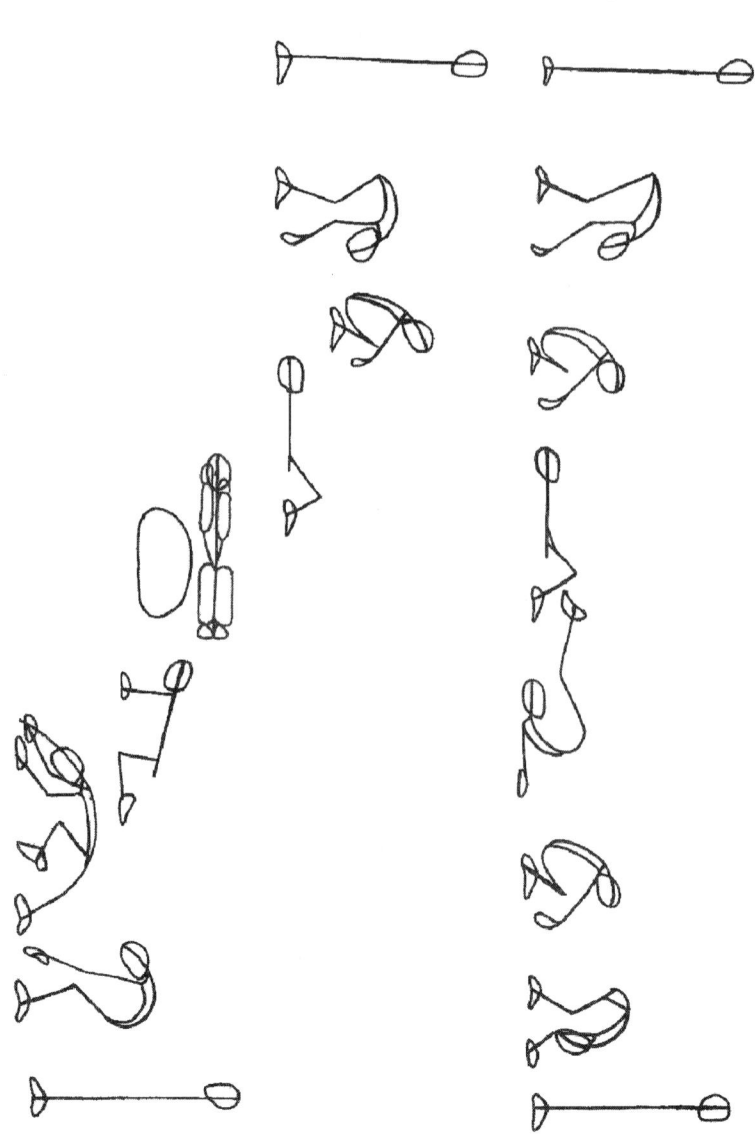

TURN AND FALL

Stand around a central vertical axis. Momentum carries body down through squatting or sitting and then out along surface of floor. Leverage comes from folding torso against hips and from balancing movement in the bottom of the torso with movement in the top of torso and head. Arms support action, easing body down to floor. Yield continuously to floor. Stand, curve and turn, bend knees, take weight on hands, and arrive lying on floor. Roll.

This action has many of the same possible movements as rolling.

Find momentum from rolling to bring body uncurving and turning to stand. Action is a continuous flow of energy, body not jerking and interrupting action. Each part of the turn and fall is accommodated and counter-balanced so that the action is smooth and continuous.

Action is circular. Back serves as a spring, spirals and circles to floor. Repeated practice brings the action into conscious thought. Work in a purposeful, calm state. There are moments of greater and lesser exertion but action continues throughout. The impulse for action continues through different energy changes. Going down is continuous with coming up and again is continuous with going down.

Standing stillness between falls retains the sense of moving. Starting action is really continuing action. Beginning action is not a break from stillness. It is a continuation of flowing energy. Easy action goes from high energy to stillness with a sense of purpose and calm.

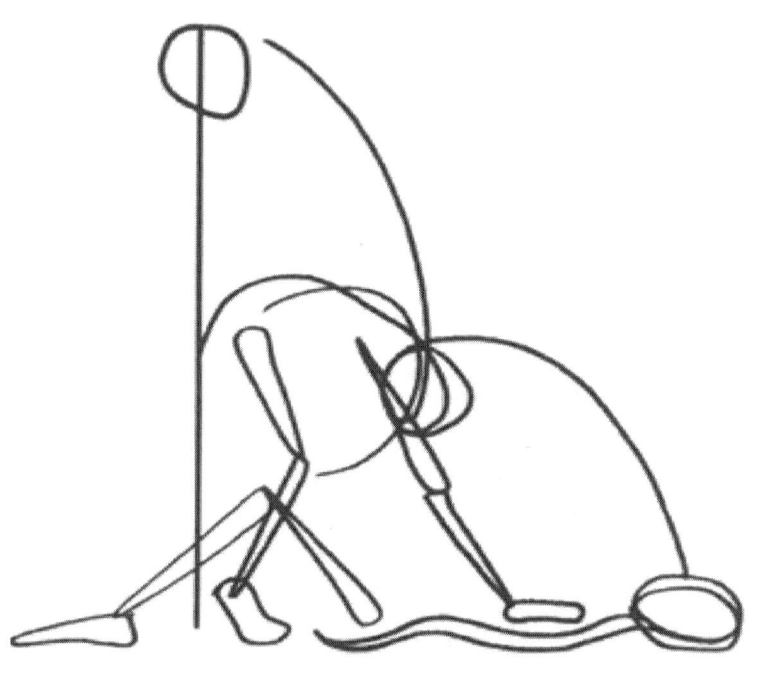

ROLL AROUND AND THROUGH AXIS

Rolling can take place around the torso by allowing different parts of the body to fall around the central axis. This is circular action, rotation in the axis.

Rolling can also take place folding through the axis of the body. Roll forward and backward. Body prepares in rest position. Legs rise upward, supported and aided by arms and hands until legs fold, thighs to chest. Action continues without stopping; knees pass over shoulders and feet meet floor. Knees continue over, bodyweight balanced on one shoulder, neck and head. Hands aid action. One knee meets floor, and body completes roll to arrive on balls of feet and palms of hands. Similar to squat but with heels lifted, body is forward and this is the first time since rest position that body has reached stillness.

Hands and arms provide support and leverage throughout roll backward. Torso folds and unfolds against thighs using leverage inside hips.

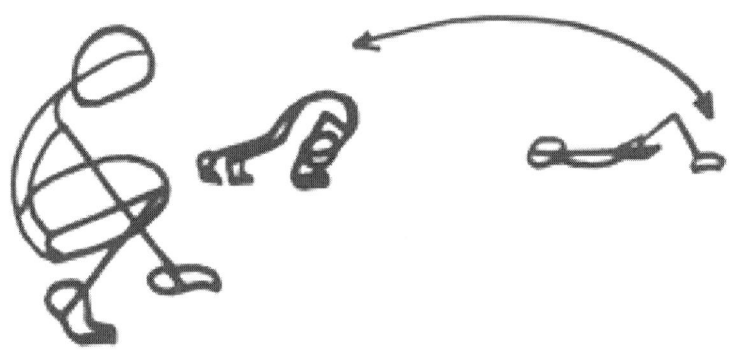

Or, rolling forward, start standing. Curving forward, hands reach floor, heels rise easily as body squats, weight is shared between hands and balls of feet. Curve forward continues, hips rise. Arms support head and shoulders moving down to meet floor. Top back of head meets floor. Curve continues in torso. Momentum carries body onto back. Hands lose contact with floor as body momentum takes over. Roll forward. Roll down whole back of torso. Curve continues and head rises up and forward. Heels leave floor, weight again rests on hands and balls of feet Uncurve to stand.

When momentum of falling body weights directs action, ease and continuity result. This is learned by repetition. Roll around and through axis. Circles and arcs throughout body.

CURVES IN ARMS

Swinging easily from shoulders, arms for arcs in space. Leverage comes from the back of torso. Momentum is created by yielding quickly to gravity, then allowing swing action which has been established to be aided and directed on the arm lift.

Stand around a central vertical axis. Arms lift to side of body, beginning action in back of torso. Let one arm drop easily across front of body. As arm passes torso, whole body follows, stepping one quarter turn around axis. Arrive facing arms lifted to front. Let arm fall back again, this time alongside of body and step back around central axis. Body returns to starting position, arms raised to side.

Continue arm swing. Allow body to respond to suggestions for possible direction changes. Action takes place in shoulder. Easy action. Allow total body participation. Small arcs or large swinging circles.

CIRCLES IN ARMS

Stand around. a central vertical axis. Lift both arms to sides of body, describing a huge arc in front of body. Arms come together until fingers touch in front of body. Arms form a circle parallel to the floor. Find support for action by lengthening down back to torso. Hands descend slowly in front of body. Arms rest again, hanging along sides of torso. Back of torso remains wide and long as arms work. Arms find other arcs around body.

Fingers of one hand seek fingers of other hand. One arm knows where other arm is completing its action. Arms used together make circles. Back curves and knees bending will allow greater recognition of possibility. Some arcs compel body movement, spreading through the whole structure.

Arms work as part of total body. Arms send information to the axis. Arms receive information from the axis. Arms send information to legs and receive information from legs. All parts of the body speak to one another through the axis. Hand knows hand through the axis. Physical knowing.

SWING LEGS AND ARMS

Stand around a central vertical axis. Whole body axis falls easily forward. Almost simultaneously leg swings forward from high inside torso. Swinging leg catches falling axis, huge step with whole foot on floor but arch lifted. Arrive in wide stride, front to back. Feet remain parallel. Whole swinging leg travels straightforward defining a plane, and whole back leg moves in its own plane of action which is parallel to that of swinging leg. Then central axis swings up to vertical, pushed by back leg. Back leg swings through to front. Axis falls forward again. Back leg swinging through becomes front leg, catching weight in front. Very huge steps. Arms and legs work oppositionally. Arm swing aids action. Knees bend easily throughout action.

Legs swing from high inside hips. Crawling, walking and running are good examples of this action which also takes place in rolling and falling. Leverage for thigh moving forward comes from the front lower half of the central axis. If thigh swings to side or back, leverage comes from hip region, more exterior to the torso, and not immediately at the central axis. Yet, the central axis serves as the stabilising factor, supporting bones of bottom of torso in turn provide leverage for leg action to side and back. The central axis is a fundamental support for all leg action.

Leverage for arms comes mainly from the back of torso, directly related to central axis. Some leverage for arm action comes from front of torso, less directly related to central axis, which is approximated by the vertebral column. However, the same situation applies as with legs. Ultimately the leverage can be traced back to the axis.

Direction of huge steps can change. Axis falls to side, diagonal, back, anywhere. Falling axis, swinging limbs.

Changing emphasis: if leg swing precedes axis falling, up and down are emphasised more than forward or through space.

Elbow and knee accommodate action by transferring movement from centre to periphery. Elbow carries a message from shoulder to hand, from hand to shoulder. Knee carries a message from hip to ankle, from ankle to hip.

TURN

Turning is like rolling. Take a series of steps which turn the body around on its axis.

Let right arm work with right leg. Let left arm work with left leg.

Central vertical axis remains upright.

Try half turns, two of which make a full circle.

Begin standing with one side of body closest to planned destination. Look over shoulder toward destination. Raise arms to sides. Take one step sideways as arms and legs both reach out to the sides of body. Enormous circle. This is the beginning position. Swing arm and leg further from destination, around body, step on that leg, completing one-half turn. Arrive looking in the same direction, over opposite shoulder, one step nearer destination.

Continue action, rotating axis in the same direction. Swing arm and leg furthest from destination around body so they become close to destination. Head continues to watch destination until last possible moment, then completes full circle to see destination again.

Keep circling the same direction to make several full circles, then do the same turning in the opposite direction.

Turning is like rolling. In turning same arm and leg work together. This is unlike the automatic action in walking and running when the opposite arm and leg work together. In actions where the rotation of the axis is required, the same arm and leg will usually work together.

Knees bend easily on each step. By deepening the folding action at knees, an easy flow down, as body takes a step, and up, as body turns, is allowed.

Momentum of swing, using inside and outside of thigh as body turns, also aids action.

Axis remains upright throughout turn, though axis travels in a straight line across space.

There are many ways to turn. Other ways may be found by changing direction in space and changing the axis of the body.

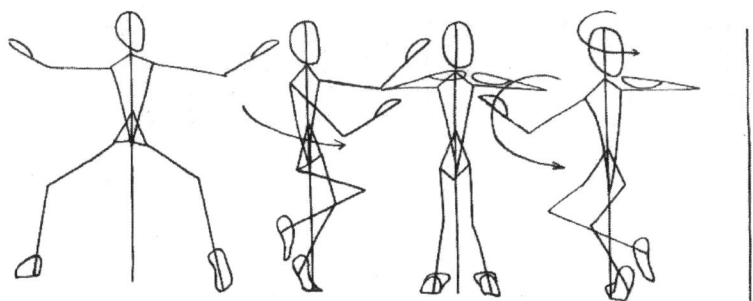

JUMP

Stand around a central vertical axis. Feet are parallel. Axis of foot is from second toe to centre of heel. These axes are parallel. Knees slide forward. Centre of knee slides over second toe. Fold at hips, knees and ankles. Both heels stay on floor. Torso remains vertical, back wide. Unfold knees, hips and ankles to return whole body to vertical standing. This is leg action for jump. Direction of leg action may change, preserving axis of hip, centre of knee, centre of ankle, second toe.

Stand around a central vertical axis. Shift weight to one side, standing on one leg but with both feet still in contact with floor. Slowly lift free heel, keeping ball of foot on floor.

Continue to push foot away from floor slowly, toes leaving floor last. Central axis supports leg as foot rises. This is a very small shift. The shift of weight to the side happens as late as possible during action so body support is shared between both feet for as long as possible. Likewise, axis falls back to centre as soon as possible. Toes return first to floor, then ball to foot, mid foot, and heel return. This is foot action for jumping.

Think of performing this action with a sense of falling to centre.

Stand around central vertical axis. Arms hang at sides of body, where they remain. Action takes place below torso, in hips and legs. Knees slide forward. Hips and ankles bend. Rapidly unfold hips, knees and ankles simultaneously, allowing ankle action to continue into foot as heels lift, middle foot, ball of foot and toes follow. Body moves directly upward, slightly forward, as weight shifts to balls of feet and into vertical axis above head.

Descending, toes meet floor, balls of feet, middle feet, then heels. Action travels up foot to ankle as heels contact floor. Then whole action, ankle, knee, hip is simultaneous. Whole body settles down around a vertical axis. Arrive at small knee bend.

IN THE JUMP

Action in legs is elastic and flows. Weight is taken through longer levers to shorter ones on the upward action, and through shorter levers to longer ones on the descent. Strongest action begins and ends jump.

Moving central axis slightly forward keeps axis over base of support. That support becomes smaller as feet leave floor. As body descends, whole centre axis moves back; base of support becomes larger as more of the foot contacts the floor. The vertical axis is always falling to the centre of the base of support.

Jump into the axis which moves slightly forward and up as body rises, and backward and down as body lands.

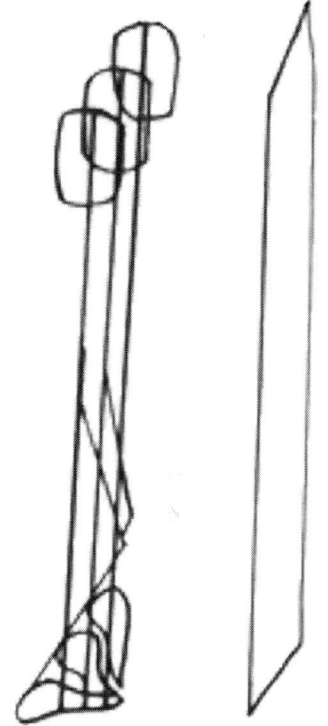

RUN AND LEAP

Run with a central vertical axis. Subtle fall and recovery. Use feet fully. Land on ball of each foot, roll down to heel. Push with heel of each foot, through whole foot to toes as foot leaves floor behind. Extend running so steps are long and broad. Body rides high between steps. Arms continue in running action. Run with one short, fast, low step and one slow, broad, high step. Repeat both sides. Action is continuously forward with torso. Body balances evenly between legs. Never a moment of panic. Time spent in the air is continuous with time spent on the floor. Purposeful, calm action.

The falling central axis provides reason for the leap. The fall allows the rise. Deepen knee bend and speed up unfolding action to gain elevation.

RUN AND TURN IN THE AIR

Run with a central vertical axis. Subtle fall, catch. Run and turn in air is related to run and leap.

Let one arm and leg swing across body while in air leaping. Rise up around the central axis and roll in the air. Turn high and as body falls land easily, running again. Knees bend on descent to absorb the shock of landing.

Hip, knee and ankle action flows through feet on upward movement. Bones of feet transfer the impact of landing through whole foot, to ankle, up lower leg to knee, across knee to upper thigh and then through hip to vertebral column. The impact of landing after any jump, leap or turn in the air is always transferred upward in this way.

Easy action comes from the harmonious working of all body parts.

PARTIAL EXCHANGE OF WEIGHT; LEAN; DRAG

Partial exchange of weight involves sharing. Consider body parts separately, having their own weight, or as compound weights having their own weights plus that of other parts being supported. Weight in parts of the body varies greatly.

Work with five limbs: legs, arms and head.

A group of people work at walking, standing, curving forward, crawling, rolling, sitting, crawling, uncurving to stand. They work until action is automatic and comfortable. Two or more people lean together so they stand as one body. Both people curve and fall at the same time. They separate as they descend.

The two people descend relative to their leaning together. Shared weight happens on the periphery of the body or at body centre. Let the idea of rolling and becoming lost in the movement itself be the guide as to when contact is possible. Work very slowly, listening. Extend leaning together by shifting supporting axis more heavily into one of the two bodies. One person becomes the main support. Supporting body gently pulls other body along floor.

Stand, lean, drag, fall.

Working in a group has its own shape. Action means only what it is. Participate in action without attaching interpretive evaluations. Become very comfortable with physicality. The body speaks of the body.

Comfortable body regards inherent shape of movement, becomes aware of infinite possibilities, rests easily into body choice.

Combine: walk, stand, curve, crawl, roll, sit, crawl, stand with stand, lean, drag, fall.

Listen to a group working situation even while being wholly inside the situation. Working comfortably allows separation from the question of 'What does it mean?' to

'What is now?' The comfortable body can consider the present situation.

THE NATURE OF PHYSICAL UNDERSTANDING

Throughout the work with others there are no other signals but the body signals. The touch is the beginning.

>Two or more people can come to physical understanding.
>No symbols.
>No power plays.
>No spoken dialogue.
>No directions.
>No seduction. No attack.
>No defense.
>Simply: Body speaks to body in the language of the axis.

Actions such as leaning, rolling together and carrying can take on a longer flow of energy by continuing one into another.

Two people remain working together as long as the impulse for action is present. This depends on a shared understanding of time between two people.

DOUBLE ROLL

A group of people roll around and through the central axis. They make contact, rolling together. Roll to stand, return to roll. Weight passes easily between two bodies, from one body to the other, as they roll together. Axial movement. Continuous flow between the two people.

Weight tells the story of its own approach, direction and departure.

Prediction goes through the body from first touch.

Roll together with another person.

CARRY

Support weight through body centre. Present axis as support as often as possible. Arms and legs share weight through axis.

Crawl on hands and knees. Roll. Crawl. Uncurve to stand. Walk. Gently and continuously give full body weight to a person crawling. Crawl and support another body across back.

Stand, torso hinged forward at hips, arms supporting torso with hands resting on thighs. Knees bend. Feet far apart. Support another body on back of torso.

Stand upright, feet apart. Knees bend, keeping feet parallel. Support another body lying across thighs. Arms help support.

Supporting person standing. Person being carried holds on to supporting person, with arms around neck, and legs around waist or hips. Supporting person uses arms under carried persons thighs to help support. Face to face or carried person on back of supporting person.

Stand facing another person. Supporting person curves forward to put shoulder into hip fold of person being carried. Person being carried curves forward, over supporting person's back.

Person supporting lifts with legs and back to arrive standing with person carried resting over one shoulder. Head and arms hang behind centre of support. Legs balance that weight in front of centre of support.

There are many simple ways to carry. All rely on balancing weight and sharing support through body using whole axis.

Person being carried takes a helpful role. By using lower arms, lower legs, feet and hands as levers it is possible to provide supporting surfaces, to be more easily carried. Holding on with hands, feet, insides and front of thighs, lower legs, lower arms, sides of arms, with head and neck – this enables person being carried to keep weight close to axis of supporting person.

All the action between two people touching is read by the two bodies and understood by each, as well as between them. Signals of direction, balance, leverage and timing can be understood physically. Physical touch communicates these signals which become the impulse for action between two people.

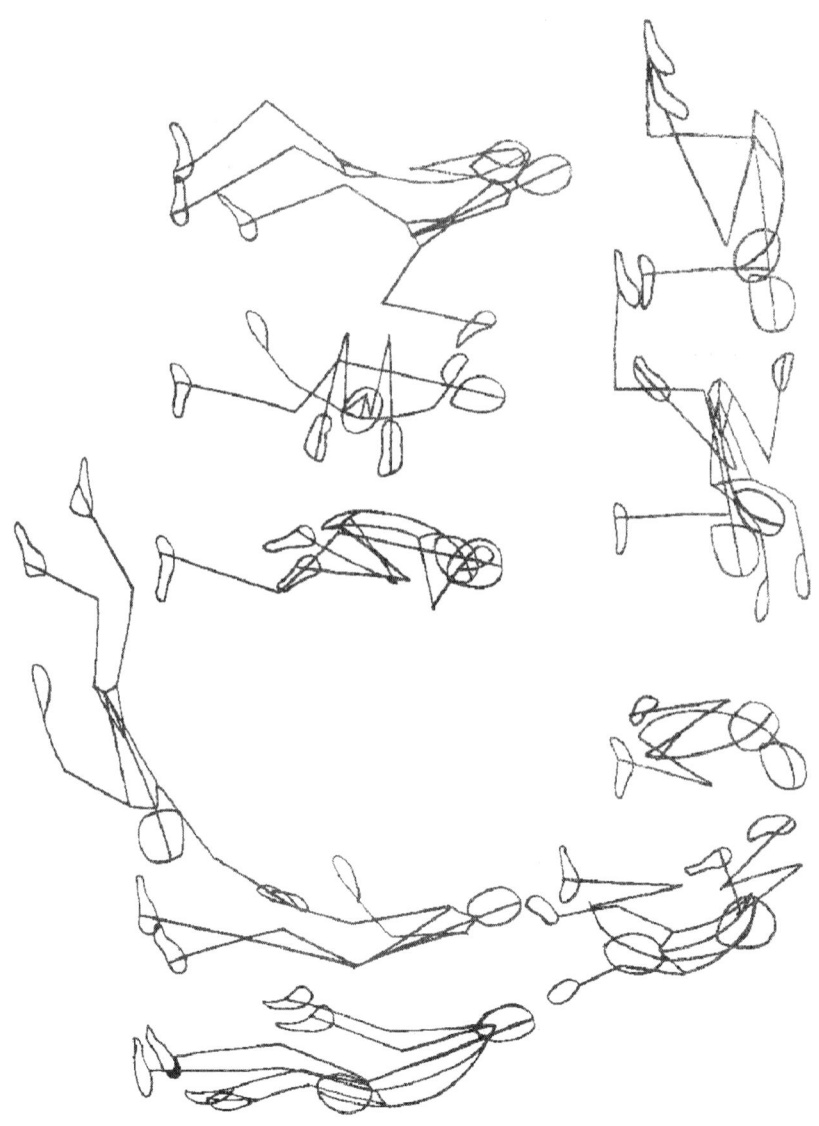

SIMPLE ACTIONS COMBINED

Consider some possibilities:
1. Roll to stand, run, turn in air, turn and fall, roll around and through the axis.
2. Walk, stand to crawl, sit back on heels.
3. Roll to sit, stillness, roll to sit, stillness. Repeat.
4. Curve and fall, roll, stillness.
5. Roll to sit, sit to crawl, sit on heels, crawl, roll. Repeat.
6. Walk, knees bend, turn, raise arm.
7. Run and leap, turn and fall.
8. Jump, curve and fall.
9. Swing arms and legs, run, turn in air, turn, stand, still balance.
10. Turn, turn and fall.
11. Knee bend, jump, knee bend, run and leap.
12. Squat, uncurve to stand, walk, run, run and leap.
13. Partial exchange of weight, stillness, carry.
14. Double roll, roll apart.
15. Roll around and through the axis, roll to stand.
16. Stand, still balance, walk.
17. Lean, curve, fall.
18. Stillness, run and turn in air, walk.
19. Walk, curves in arms.
20. Partial exchange of weight, fall, roll, run.
21. Turn to fall, roll.
22. Stillness, still balance.
23. Carry, run.
24. Carry, stillness, partial exchange of weight, curve, uncurve to stand, run.

Combined simple actions are treated as situations. They may be regarded as complete in themselves or developed into larger units. Become lost in a simple series of actions.

PART THREE: SEEING A CONTEXT

USING THE IMAGE IN ACTION

My dances are composed of situations in a whole context which are designed to allow for work on an intuitive level: a spontaneous release of energy which expresses what the performers and I do. Any piece may vary in outward appearance during different performances but the context and situations are understood and their definitions separate the sections and the piece from others.

The meaning of any one performance is related to all the times that the piece has been performed as well as to the fact of it being new in itself. The accumulation of past experiences, as well as directions or indications for further work, are part of the structure. The meaning is in the moment. Definition of situation and then definition of context are my jobs as a dance maker.

When I go to the ocean and see the line where the water meets the sky, I walk on that line, over it, across it, floating, stepping carefully, sometimes in water, sometimes in air. With my new body I can step into air or water without being dropped or drowned. I open my arms and become that line. Half of me is water, half air. I am cold. I put on a sweater.

Working with these ideas, my dancers find a body state in which they become the images of the story. The gesture does not pretend to tie the story. Accepting being the story comes before any gesture. Deep participation in the image yields the process. Deep participation yields the inside of the image from which the body state is formed. A dance about walking need not involve walking, but it may. Whether or not it does becomes incidental.

GROUP WORKING

When I work with a group and I see something that interests me, I try to describe that back into the group as they work. In this way the group becomes aware of the outside of what is happening as well as the inside. Also, I suggest possible directions. And so we work. Gradually the work becomes defined. The shape emerges. If the result is inconsistent with the original intention, I don't mind. I am apt to abandon any idea at any time. I look for a progression of ideas which then finds its own way.

After many sessions of definition, a series of situations becomes crystalised. They vary according to the type of definition which has been derived. For example, taking just one parameter of definition, a few ways duration can be defined:
- a watch
- physical fatigue
- steps on a ladder
- eating time
- length of hair
- boiling water
- shoe size
- Declaration of Independence
- number of repetitions
- a flashing light
- a wandering insect.

Hopefully the length of a section is a result of knowing either what the material is and how it needs to be defined or what definition is and how it wants to serve.

With a series of events, some with specific lengths, others variable, I make a dance.

Usually parts are grouped by further definitions. Proportion is always a factor. In the end, proportion of space and time are my primary concerns. Energy becomes the vehicle.
Physicality makes the statement.

In this work there are no mistakes, but there is growth. Performers grow to understand complex possibilities. They learn to exploit their choices. They are encouraged to work in response to a total situation.

There exists a persistent dialogue between patient waiting and demand. One finds the balance between inner rest and desire to act, and this balance is tenuous because the ability to wait and to demand does not always increase in direct proportion to each other.

The dancer listens to their own rhythm.
The dancer listens to the rhythm of the whole space.
The dancer hears all the parts alone and together.
The dancer makes a part from what she or he hears.

Output takes the form of choice making when performers are aware of many possibilities and direct their attention toward any one or few of them.

SEEING CHANGE

I had repeated the action so many times and each successive time I gave over more. I drew inward with my attention so I was unaware of other people in the same place. I felt myself falling and sitting, falling and sitting. The bones in my back unfolded and opened each time I sat.
    I saw the boards open and I fell through the floor and sat up floating sideways out of the window. I got a drink of water. When I returned I fell softly down, not being able to walk on the floor as it was opening and closing.
    I was unafraid and I rested. When I woke there were sounds outside the window, birds singing, people walking by talking.

REPETITION

Repetition is important It allows the image to go through plateaus of recognition. The image falls through the body and becomes real.
    I listen to my breathing without interfering.
    On the breath-out, I let the image become clear.
    On the breath-in, I let the image escape.
    Empty waiting goes into highly concentrated, centred attention.

FINDING A QUESTION

Expectations prevent the performer from responding to the total situation. As the situation changes, so do the possibilities. A performer must not unknowingly persist in an expectation which is based upon a past situation.

The process of finding a question is very compelling. When I ask a question about my material I am defining my relationship to it. So, the dimensions that the question takes are fundamental to my work. In a sense I look for questions rather than for answers, and I let the questions throw me into further work. I then find new questions and so begin again. This may sound futile but, in actual fact, it yields a progression of thoughts which, though related, is varied, flexible and self-propelling. The results of my work embody the suggestions of answers I have found. Once I see such suggestions I am eager to indicate them (like I see what time of day it is), so that I can get on with other questions. I want to choreograph a series of suggestions.

To want to choreograph a series of suggestions has led me into a rich questioning of what is a possibility and what is an actuality.

As a result of this, some pieces turn out to be finished when they are at a stage of development where many other choreographers seem to begin. For me that's fine, because I am interested in letting my work suggest possibilities, while retaining options in interpretation. For a person to see my dances, he or she is allowed to develop an individual route through the material. There is no one way to see it. For me, it's a matter of clarifying multiple directions, layered thinking.

Once a process, feeling state or thought is crystalized, it becomes complete. Being in the centre of an idea allows it to be. One of my students did a spontaneous dance. I asked her if she could repeat it. She said "Yes", and danced again. I asked her what was repeated and she said, "I worked until I was entirely done each time". Was it the same dance – totally different in outward appearance? I think it was. The one element of the piece which became important in the first doing was clearly repeated. Clarity resides in many forms.

THE IMPOSSIBLE QUESTION

An important feature of my work is that I am always looking for questions which demand a creative leap to find an answer. A question of contradiction or impossibility often becomes a beginning. Very often understandings occur outside usual verbal definitions. An apparent contradiction often becomes a coherent statement of feeling or sensation, even without resolving the verbal level of expression:
    a silent harmony
    a puzzle without pieces
    a moving stillness.

THE IMAGE BECOMES LIGHT

The image falls through the body, deeper and deeper, and then it gets light and spacious. It is present without effort. The image suggests movement.

REVEALING INTENTION

Transparency is a quality which is present when people are moving with full mind and body concentration upon the physicality of any moment. There is no room for extravagance in this concentration, extravagance implying disproportion or excess over need, because transparency is a single unity. Need demands fulfilment, nothing more, nothing less. Direct contact of mind and body are revealed. Energy is seen naked. It is not the personality alone which becomes visible. It is the total mind and body self. When mind and body are united the result is a very simple, direct expression of intention. One can see through the whole person to find this intention. The person becomes transparent.

CENTRED THINKING

One comes to a deep understanding of an image by allowing it to become the main focus of both mental and physical thought. Participation in an image can be enormous. It is this participation which allows the total body clarity which is transparent.

LEARNING TO USE IMAGES IN DANCES

First I see it. I recognise the image. I begin to feel it with my other ideas and it remains strange, separate from me.

Then I think it. I begin to let the image fall through the body. I apply the image to myself.

Then I forget it. I have thought it enough so that the body knows. The image becomes a body state, a total situation. The image has fallen through the body.

Then it happens. The body and the image become the same thing. There is no separation. Mind and body are in harmony. No longer is it an image. There is total participation.

(A child told Mabel Todd, "First you see it, then you think it, then you forget it, then it happens." Barbara Clark told me this. Mabel Ellsworth Todd, *The Thinking Body* and Barbara Clark, *Living in Your Axis* and *Body Proportion Needs Depth*.)

EXPECTATIONS

Directions to dancers: "Lose expectations which are only relevant to the moment of their creation. Allow easy dialogue to result by making plans which allow context to develop. Formulate from a given moment for that moment only. Persistence in expectation causes rigidity, lack of alertness to the moment. Listen when working. Make an atmosphere from which to choose the parts of this moment."

INDEPENDENT ACTION AND UNISON

Everybody can be learning the same thing using different outwardly visible gestures. The same idea or image can have multiple realizations, prismatic effects. Also, it is sometimes important to achieve the outward appearance of unity. In working, this provides for objective clarity.

Many images may occur in the same place and at the same time.

MORE ADVANCED WORK

In advanced work one holds a complex set of body images, specific skills which constantly develop and enrich movement possibilities, and is available for contact with others at any time. One is available for imagined journeys which change, enrich and feed the working process. These things are all held as absences within the body. One waits as if empty through the whole process of this work and it is such availability that allows for the recognition of possibility This sense of absence is not passive. It has to do with the recognition of multiple possibilities. Even when initiating action or responding to the recognition of possibility, more than one idea is generated and then used, either kept or dropped.

There is a state of readiness – not having already decided – which enables one to see potential development in a situation. This empty state is very active. Being absent in this way is being fully present.

In advanced ensemble work a group of people are empty together with the possibilities of a given situation, including the flow of energy between people in space and time. All are absent in the sense of being available, not ego entertained, but ready, responsive. All are fully present in the sense of listening, answering, asking and showing by doing.

TOWARDS CONTACT

When one person is working and another person approaches, the person working alone must be available for the duet to happen immediately. Both people already hold the possibility of dancing with others as well as dancing alone. Duets form and end easily as part of the work. There is a physical preparation for contact. At an advanced level one is ready to meet the world of the dance. This happens easily and graciously, without special attention. A meeting must not be demanded and can only be offered. If it is not accepted, a meeting must never be insisted upon. To keep the work relevant the attention must remain centred upon what is happening at the moment. Any delay in giving up expectations as they become less relevant means the process of contact is in danger of becoming manipulative. The persons see the evolving context and allow participation in every moment of that context as it evolves.

A COMPLEX BODY IMAGE

Directions to dancers: "Consider each of the spinal bones separately, starting at the top, proceeding downwards. On the breaths-out, begin to isolate 33 separate places in the vertebral column. Consider the pre-fused sacrum. On the breaths-in, let the image rest. Initially this is experienced as a cycle of 33 breaths with attention focused on 33 consecutive positions descending the back of the body. Later one finds it possible to gain information from the body as to weight, mobility, size and shape of vertebrae. One finds in listening to the body that information is given and verified. The nature of the information is experience and sensation. This process is repeated many times.

Next, consider any substance found in nature. Repeat aloud the name of that substance on each breath out, on each vertebra. Let the two images merge, supporting bones and natural substance, creating a new kind of imaginary support for the body. One actually believes and becomes the image. There can be no pretending because one either is able to centre attention completely or else is unable to find the image. One always knows to what degree one has been successful in capturing the image as it, in turn, captures its creator. Let movement come from the new body support. One must stop the process and begin again if loss of concentration is experienced. It is important to remain patient, going slowly through the thought process. It is enough to be still and establish a cycle of 33 breaths descending the back. One need do no more than what is easy. This work is about comfort, being with, rather than against, oneself."

GROUP DANCE FROM THE SAME IMAGE

"Consider how your substance is found in relation to others in nature. Dances of common materials meeting, shared between people, having the rhythms of their breaths:

    grass and apple
    wood and spider web
    acorn and grass
    wood and leaf
    stone and moss."

QUESTIONS FOR DANCERS

Make a white gesture, filled with suggestions, hesitating,
Clarifying the word 'absence' to mean
A moment of dense implication.

———————

Dance the interior air space
       rhythmic,
       opening,
       becoming smaller,
       cellular,
       with a shape that changes,
       with walls that are porous,
       dark,
       private.

———————

Wait for the wind.
The wind comes.
Become the wind.
       A dance in three parts.

———————

Duet with yourself and light.

———————

Air through,
and through,
and through,
and through,
and through
       the whole body.

———————

Breathe up and down in the centre of the air
Let an image of the action come to mind.
Up and down.
Dance with the image of action and breath combined.

dew ---- mist
wide ---- south

_____

Dance time of shoulder and knee.
Dance time of a stick thrown in air.
Dance the meeting of two of the earth's surfaces.

_____

Pass through a space as though you are walking behind yourself.
Follow the image of yourself.
Precede the image of yourself.

_____

Expand the space between moving and being still.
    Begin moving one part of the body.
    Let movement gradually flow throughout the whole body. Go
    so gradually into moving that stillness prevails.
    Stop so suddenly that movement continues.
    Stop suddenly but think movement goes on.
    Wake up in the morning already moving.

_____

Dream stillness while running.
Dream running while standing still.
I dream I am a run.

_____

Dance a moving stillness.

_____

Listen to breath.
Breathe in a narrow column in the body centre.
Deepen the breath out, open the back of the throat, and yawn.

Yawn a deep sound.
Follow the sound into movement.

Be easy on yourself.
The breath supports the movement.

Two people together dance a shared yawn.

Dance with a physical voice.

Dance with another person so your energies follow one path.
You listen together.

Dance in a group, walking in and out of sunlight, gathering energy, but not wasting any.

Dance in a group: carry, lean, rest, watch, crawl, roll, fall, run, stand.

A group of people:
    Stand in a circle.
    Imagine a door in your life;
        a real door
        a problem with an answer, known or unknown,
        an opening through,
        any door.
    Consider the nature of the door.
    Dance the opening of the door and passage through.

A group of people:
    Stand in a circle.
    Imagine a door in your life.
    Consider.
    Dance the opening and passage through.
    Dance the next door which presents itself after your passage through the first door.
    Pass through five doors, each considered as a result of passage through the one before.
    Let one of the passages bring you into contact with another person.
    Wait in stillness until the room becomes still with you.
    This is about the body state of passage through the interior.

A group of people
    Stand in a line.
    Remember a path you have taken in your life.
    Change to a new place in relation to the line of beginning, using the remembered journey as an indication for how you move to the new place.
    Memory gives rise to responsive movement possibility.

A white bird circling below me to the right,
Spiralling down and away – another prey.
Seen after the thin sliver of moon in daylight.

_____

On a pier going outward.
A woman climbs a ladder to reach me from a houseboat She has hair like my friend, but red.
She gives me a feather about ten inches long, shaped like a flat fish.
All the parts separate, blowing in a gentle wind.

_____

She asks me will I come to her boat.
I want to go and see the rest of the pier.
We ask questions without speaking.
I wonder if she wants her feather back.
She doesn't
We understand goodbye and I leave.

_____

In making dances if you don't see the reason for the inclusion of any material, but you feel it to be essential, consider such material.

Spring/Summer 1976

Also available from Triarchy Press

Linda Hartley
Embodied Spirit, Conscious Earth ~ Linda Hartley

Miranda Tufnell
A Widening Field ~ Miranda Tufnell & Chris Crickmay
Body Space Image ~ Miranda Tufnell & Chris Crickmay
When I Open My Eyes: dance health imagination ~ Miranda Tufnell

Sandra Reeve: Ways of Being a Body
Body and Awareness ~ ed. Sandra Reeve
Nine Ways of Seeing a Body ~ Sandra Reeve
Body and Performance ~ ed. Sandra Reeve

Skinner Releasing Technique
Skinner Releasing Technique: A Movement and Dance Practice ~ Manny Emslie

Alexander Technique
Before the Curtain Opens: Alexander Technique in the Actor's Life ~ Kate Kelly

Amerta Movement
The Roots of Amerta Movement ~ Lise Lavelle
Embodied Lives ~ ed. Katya Bloom, Margit Galanter & Sandra Reeve

Somatics and Ecosomatics
Rock Songs: story about walk about story about walkabout story ~ Nick Sales
Suomenlinna | Gropius: Two Contemplations on Body, Movement and Intermateriality ~ Paula Kramer
Attending to Movement ~ ed. Sarah Whatley, Natalie Garrett Brown & Kirsty Alexander
Nature Connection ~ Margaret Kerr and Jana Lemke

www.triarchypress.net/movement

About *Theatre Papers*

Language of the Axis was first published in **Theatre Papers** as a loose leaf book so that dancers might respond in movement to the provocations within a particular page and photograph.

Theatre Papers (1977-1986), was a documentation project conceived and run by Peter Hulton. Begun at Dartington College of Arts, it grew to consist of 57 papers by individual practitioners, with the intention of focusing on a detailed relationship between practice and theory. *Performing Arts Journal* (New York, 1979) identified the series as being "especially valuable not only for the issues they discuss but as models of theatre criticism, in which theory is consistently related to practical example and experience, with ease and skill."

The series was later to inform the creation of the international journal *Performance Research*. After the first Council of Europe workshop on Theatre and Communities, held at Dartington in 1986, and with the arrival of portable and discrete audio-visual documentary equipment enabling a close perceptual attention to the processes and principles at work within performing arts practice, the project developed into **ARTS ARCHIVES**.

Between 1988 and 2015 **ARTS ARCHIVES** produced over one hundred DVD-ROMs of practitioners at work, a number of which were published by Methuen, Routledge, *The Drama Review* and The Open University. This material was later to form the backbone of the Routledge Performance Archive. All the material has been placed in the British Library, in the Exeter Digital Archives of Performance Practice at Exeter University and is at www.peterhulton.org.uk